DYING
TO BE ME

Hay House Titles of Related Interest

YOU CAN HEAL YOUR LIFE, the movie,
starring Louise L. Hay & Friends
(available as a 1-DVD program and an expanded 2-DVD set)
Watch the trailer at: **www.LouiseHayMovie.com**

THE SHIFT, the movie,
starring Dr. Wayne W. Dyer
(available as a 1-DVD program and an expanded 2-DVD set)
Watch the trailer at: **www.DyerMovie.com**

THE AMAZING POWER OF DELIBERATE INTENT:
Living the Art of Allowing, by Esther and Jerry Hicks

"LIFE WAS NEVER MEANT TO BE A STRUGGLE," by Stuart Wilde

PEACE FROM BROKEN PIECES: How to Get Through
What You're Going Through, by Iyanla Vanzant

A SURVIVOR'S GUIDE TO KICKING CANCER'S ASS,
by Dena Mendes

TRAVELING AT THE SPEED OF LOVE, by Sonia Choquette

WISHES FULFILLED: Mastering the Art of Manifesting,
by Dr. Wayne W. Dyer

YOU CAN CREATE AN EXCEPTIONAL LIFE,
by Louise Hay and Cheryl Richardson

All of the above are available at your local bookstore,
or may be ordered by visiting:

Hay House USA: **www.hayhouse.com**®
Hay House Australia: **www.hayhouse.com.au**
Hay House UK: **www.hayhouse.co.uk**
Hay House South Africa: **www.hayhouse.co.za**
Hay House India: **www.hayhouse.co.in**

DYING
TO BE ME

MY JOURNEY FROM CANCER,
TO NEAR DEATH,
TO TRUE HEALING

ANITA
MOORJANI

HAY HOUSE, INC.
Carlsbad, California • New York City
London • Sydney • Johannesburg
Vancouver • Hong Kong • New Delhi

Published and distributed in the United States by: Hay House, Inc.: www
.hayhouse.com® • *Published and distributed in Australia by:* Hay House Australia Pty. Ltd.: www.hayhouse.com.au • *Published and distributed in the United
Kingdom by:* Hay House UK, Ltd.: www.hayhouse.co.uk • *Published and distributed in the Republic of South Africa by:* Hay House SA (Pty), Ltd.: www.hayhouse
.co.za • *Distributed in Canada by:* Raincoast: www.raincoast.com • *Published in
India by:* Hay House Publishers India: www.hayhouse.co.in

Cover design: Christy Salinas • *Interior design:* Pam Homan

Library of Congress Cataloging-in-Publication Data

Moorjani, Anita.
  Dying to be me : my journey from cancer, to near death, to true healing / Anita
Moorjani. -- 1st ed.
      p. cm.
  ISBN 978-1-4019-3751-5 (hardback)
  1. Moorjani, Anita, 1959---Health. 2. Cancer--Patients--Biography. 3. Cancer--
Psychological aspects. I. Title.
  RC262.M664 2012
  362.196'9940092--dc23
  [B]

                              2011042365

Hardcover ISBN: 978-1-4019-3751-5
Digital ISBN: 978-1-4019-3752-2

15 14 13 12   4 3 2 1
1st edition, March 2012

Printed in the United States of America

To Danny, my true love: I've always known that our love extends beyond time and space. If not for you, I wouldn't be here in this physical life today.

To my dear mother, and my wonderful brother, Anoop: Thank you for being there for me through my life, but most especially though my illness, and caring for me when I needed you most. I wish everyone had a family who cared about them the way you care about me.

In memory of my dear father, whose biggest dream was to see my wedding, but who left this realm before the big day: Thank you for giving me the opportunity to experience your infinite presence and unconditional love in the other realm, and for assuring me that you're here, there, and everywhere.

I believe that the greatest truths of the universe don't lie outside, in the study of the stars and the planets. They lie deep within us, in the magnificence of our heart, mind, and soul. Until we understand what is within, we can't understand what is without.

I share my story here in the hope of touching your heart in some way and reminding you of your own magnificence.

Contents

❧ *Foreword* ❧

I have been deeply and profoundly touched by the contents of this book, and even more so by my personal relationship with Anita Moorjani, who came into my life through a series of Divinely orchestrated coincidences. For more than four years, an advancing cancer brought Anita to death's doorstep and beyond—inside the house of death itself, way beyond the doorway and the entrance hall, if you will. Anita has described it all in great detail in this soul-searching book. I encourage you to read it very carefully and thoughtfully with a mind that's open to having many of your cherished beliefs challenged, especially about what lies beyond this world, in what's often called the *hereafter.*

Surrounded by loved ones and a medical team anticipating her last breath at any moment, Anita lay in a deep coma. Yet she was given the opportunity to return to her cancer-ravaged body, defying all odds, and experience incredible healing—through the vehicle of unconditional love. More than this, she was allowed to return from the chamber of death and report to all of us what life on the other side of this corporeal world looks like—and of even more significance, *feels* like.

This is a love story—a big, unconditional love story that will give you a renewed sense of who you truly are, why you're here, and how you can transcend any fear and self-rejection that defines your life. Anita speaks with uncommon candor about her cancer, explaining why she believes she had to go down this treacherous road in her life, why she feels she was healed, and why she returned. And make no mistake about it, her life's mission is in a very big way reflected in the fact that you're about to read her report of this experience . . . and that I'm so involved in helping to get this crucial message out to the world.

What Anita discovered during her 24-hour coma when she passed through the doorway into the *other realm* is remarkably aligned with all that I've been receiving in inspired moments of writing and speaking. It's clear to both of us that Divine intervention took over and moved the pieces around in such a way that this woman living on the other side of the world, in a culture quite dissimilar from my own, was escorted into my awareness and my physical life.

I first heard of Anita when I received a copy of her near-death experience (NDE) interview from a woman in New York named Mira Kelley, who later became a friend and did a past-life regression on me (which is published in my book *Wishes Fulfilled*.) After one reading of Anita's NDE report, I felt irresistibly called to do all that I could within my limited power to get her compelling message out to the world. I called Reid Tracy, the president of Hay House, and urged him to find Anita Moorjani and ask her to write a book detailing her experience in-depth. I added that I would be pleased—no, *honored*—to write the Foreword to her book if she was willing to move ahead with it. Through a series of wonderful synchronicities—including Anita calling from Hong Kong into my weekly radio show on **hayhouseradio.com**, and my interviewing her for the entire planet to hear—we connected on both a professional and a personal level.

Anita spoke of the sense that we're all pure love. We're not only connected to everyone else and to God, but at a deeper level, we all *are* God. We've allowed our fears and ego to edge God out of our lives, which has much to do with all of the disease not only in our bodies, but in our world as well. She spoke of learning to treasure our magnificence and live as beings of light and love, and of the healing properties inherent in such a mind-set.

Anita described actually experiencing the absence of time and space, and feeling for the first time the wonder of knowing that oneness isn't an intellectual concept, but that truly everything is happening at once. She recounted being bathed in an aura of pure, blissful love, and how such a feeling has unlimited potential for healing. She learned firsthand the true meaning of the words of Jesus, that "with God all things are possible"—and that leaves *nothing* out, including healing the past. Anita discovered in person what I'd been writing about so extensively in *Wishes Fulfilled:* that in the true presence of the God-realized, the laws of the material (including the medical) world do not apply.

I had to meet this woman. Beginning with our phone conversations, I started to feel directly the spiritual essence of Anita and her message of hope as a replacement for fear. I invited her to not only write this book, but also to appear with me on PBS and tell her story of love, hope, and healing to the entire world.

I sent Anita's NDE interview to my mother, who's 95 years old and resides in an assisted-living center. My mom sees death quite frequently, since many of her new friends of advanced age simply pass away in their sleep and are gone from her experience forever. I've had many conversations with her about her thoughts on the great mystery called death that's the destiny of all living things. All that materializes *dematerializes.* We know this intellectually, yet what awaits us is still the great mystery.

After reading Anita's NDE report, my mother said that a wave of peace overtook her and replaced the fear, anxiety, and stress of what the great unknown brings. In fact, everyone who read of Anita's near-death experience, including my children, felt that they had a new lease on life and vowed to me to always, above all else, love themselves, to treasure their magnificence, and to banish all potential disease-producing thoughts from their daily lives. While I'd been writing about these ideas, Anita had brought it all home in the world of experience.

Anita was able to heal her body and told me on many occasions that she felt she came back to teach this simple but powerful lesson, which could not only heal you, but transform our world as well. And this, I know, is why God brought Anita and me together. I've always felt that it was my dharma to teach people about their own divinity and know that the highest place within them is God. We are not these bodies; we're neither our accomplishments nor our possessions—we are all one with the Source of all being, which is God. While I was writing all of this in *Wishes Fulfilled,* Anita Moorjani came into my life as if to place an exclamation point on all that I was receiving in my automatic writing. She lived it and said it so beautifully—and now you're blessed to be able to read and apply all that Anita came to know in her furious bout with advanced cancer, and her tranquil journey back through the direct experience of Divine healing.

I'm honored to play a small role in bringing this hopeful message of love as the ultimate healing. May you take Anita's words and become an instrument of removing any and all disease from your body, your relationships, your country, and our world. As Elizabeth Barrett Browning once observed poetically: "Earth's crammed with heaven, and every common bush afire with God." Indeed, healing and heaven on Earth are yours for the loving.

Enjoy Anita's wonderful, wonderful book. I love it, and I love her.

— **Dr. Wayne W. Dyer**
Maui, Hawaii

✑ *Introduction* ✑

The main purpose of sharing my story is so that others do not have to go through what I went through.

It's not my style to overtly teach people or tell them how to live their lives, nor do I like advising anyone on what changes they need to make, even if they ask. I prefer to lead by example, and create a safe environment for others to get in touch with their own truth.

I've thought about this often since the events of the winter and spring of 2006, when I had a near-death experience (NDE) and was also healed of the cancer I'd had for the previous four years. During my NDE, I was able to see and perceive certain aspects of my future life, and I understood that one of the reasons I chose to come back to earthly life was because my experience and message would touch others.

In that state, I somehow knew that in some way, I was meant to inspire thousands, maybe tens of thousands. But it wasn't clear how I was meant to do so—I just knew that in some way, I was going to be helping a lot of people. I specifically got the feeling that I didn't need to do anything for this to happen; I just had to be myself and enjoy life, and to allow myself to be an instrument for something much greater to take place.

That has been the case, as I've come to speak and write about my experiences in response to queries from the fields of medicine and science, as well as individuals seeking answers about the nature of the world and their experiences. That's how this book came to be as well (those details are in Chapter 14). I freely explain what I've learned as a result of the cancer and my NDE. I enjoy sharing my experience, and my understanding of life that I derived from it, especially when I feel that others can benefit.

My story begins in Part I, with how I grew up at the intersection of multiple cultures that held distinct and often contradictory beliefs. I'll explain how this shaped me and fostered the fears that turned out to manifest in disease, taking you with me on my journey into adulthood and my descent into the prison of cancer.

Part II explores the NDE itself—what I experienced and understood at the time—and what happened next. Being healed of cancer and working to find my new place in the world has been a surprising, challenging, and exhilarating journey!

In Part III, I'll describe what I now understand about healing, the way the world is today, and how we can live as a reflection of who we really are, allowing our magnificence to shine through. Then I'll wrap up with a question-and-answer section, containing some of the most common and most challenging concerns I hear.

But before I share with you what I've learned from my experience, I'd like to clarify that I'm not claiming to know any universal or scientific truths or to be anyone's spiritual guru. Nor am I trying to start yet another religion or belief system. My only aim is to *help,* not *convince.*

I especially wish to emphasize that you do *not* need to have an NDE to heal! My intention is to share with you all the emotional and psychological triggers that I believe contributed to my getting cancer, in the hope that in identifying these factors, you can reduce or possibly even eliminate your chances of getting sick in the first place. At the same time, if you or someone you know has cancer or any other serious illness, please know that there are many paths to healing. I would only suggest that you follow what feels right for you and resonates with you personally.

If you're looking for step-by-step instructions or a set of tenets to follow, then I'm the wrong person for you, because I don't believe in creating any "one size fits all" dogma. It would only limit who you are. Even when I speak of loving myself, my intention isn't to draw attention to me, but for you to experience that same feeling within yourself. In sharing my experience and my insights, my only purpose is to ignite the spark of magnificence that lies within you. My desire is to awaken the dormant guru within you that guides you to find your own place at the center of the universe.

It's my hope that you find joy in each and every day of your journey and come to love life as much as I do these days!

PART I

SEEKING THE RIGHT WAY

The Day I "Died"

Oh my God, I feel <u>incredible</u>! I'm so free and light! How come I'm not feeling any more pain in my body? Where has it all gone? Hey, why does it seem like my surroundings are moving away from me? But I'm not scared! Why am I not scared? Where has my fear gone? Oh wow, I can't find the fear anymore!

These were some of my thoughts as I was being rushed to the hospital. The world around me started to appear surreal and dreamlike, and I could feel myself slip farther and farther away from consciousness and into a coma. My organs were beginning to shut down as I succumbed to the cancer that had ravaged—no, devoured—my body for the past four years.

It was February 2, 2006, a day that will be etched in my memory forever as the day I "died."

Although in a coma, I was acutely aware of everything that was happening around me, including the sense of urgency and emotional frenzy of my family as they rushed me to the hospital. When we arrived, the moment the oncologist saw me, her face filled with shock.

"Your wife's heart may still be beating," she told my husband, Danny, "but, she's not really in there. It's too late to save her."

Who is the doctor talking about? I wondered. *I've never felt better in my life! And why do Mum and Danny look so frightened and worried? Mum, please don't cry. What's wrong? Are you crying because of me? Don't cry! I'm fine, really, dear Mama, I am!*

I thought I was speaking those words aloud, but nothing came out. I had no voice.

I wanted to hug my mother, comfort her and tell her that I was fine, and I couldn't comprehend why I was unable to do so. Why was my physical body not cooperating? Why was I just lying there, lifeless and limp, when all I wanted to do was to hug my beloved husband and mother, assuring them that I was fine and no longer in pain?

Look, Danny—I can move around without my wheelchair. This feels so amazing! And I'm not connected to the oxygen tank anymore. Oh wow, my breathing is no longer labored, and my skin lesions are gone! They're no longer weeping and painful. After four agonizing years, I'm finally healed!

I was in a state of pure joy and jubilation. Finally, I was free from the pain caused by the cancer that had ravaged my body. I wanted them to be happy for me. Why weren't they happy that my struggle was finally over, that *their* struggle was over? Why weren't they sharing my jubilation? Couldn't they see the joy I was feeling?

"Please, there must be something you can do," Danny and my mother pleaded with the doctor.

"It's only a matter of hours for her," the oncologist argued. "Why didn't your other doctors send her to us earlier? Her organs are already shutting down, and that's why she has slipped into a coma. She won't even make it through the night. You're asking for the impossible. Whatever we administer at this stage could prove too toxic and fatal for her body, as her organs aren't even functioning!"

"Well, maybe," Danny insisted, "but I'm not giving up on her!"

My husband held my limp hand tightly as I lay there, and I was aware of the combination of anguish and helplessness in his voice. I wanted more than anything to relieve him of his suffering. I wanted him to know how wonderful I was feeling, but I felt helpless in trying to convey it.

Don't listen to the doctor, Danny; please don't listen to her! Why is she saying that? I'm still here, and I'm fine. Better than fine—in fact, I feel great!

I couldn't understand why, but I experienced what everyone was going through—both my family members as well as the doctor. I could actually feel their fear, anxiety, helplessness, and despair. It was as though their emotions were mine. It was as though I became them.

I'm feeling your pain, darling—I can feel all your emotions. Please don't cry for me, and tell Mum not to cry for me, either. Please tell her!

But as soon as I started to get emotionally attached to the drama taking place around me, I also felt myself being simultaneously pulled away, as though there were a bigger picture, a grander plan that was unfolding. I could feel my attachment to the scene receding as I began to realize that everything was perfect and going according to plan in the greater tapestry.

It was then that the realization truly set in that I was actually dying.

Ohh . . . I'm dying! Is this what it feels like? It's nothing like I ever imagined. I feel so beautifully peaceful and calm . . . and I feel healed at last!

I then understood that even if my physical body stopped, everything is still perfect in the greater tapestry of life, for we never truly die.

I was still acutely aware of every detail unfolding before me as I observed the medical team wheeling my near-lifeless body to the intensive care unit. They were surrounding me in an emotional frenzy, hooking me up to machines while poking and prodding with needles and tubes.

I felt no attachment to my limp body as it lay there on the hospital bed. It didn't feel as though it were mine. It looked far too small and insignificant to house what I was experiencing. I felt free, liberated, and magnificent! Every pain, ache, sadness, and sorrow was gone. I was completely unencumbered, and I couldn't recall feeling this way before—not ever.

I then had a sense of being encompassed by something that I can only describe as pure, unconditional love, but even the word *love* doesn't do it justice. It was the deepest kind of caring, and I'd never experienced it before. It was beyond any physical form of affection that we can imagine, and it was *unconditional*—this was *mine*, regardless of what I'd ever done. I didn't have to do anything or behave a certain way to deserve it. This love was for me, no matter what!

I felt completely bathed and renewed in this energy, and it made me feel as though I *belonged*, as though I'd finally arrived after all those years of struggle, pain, anxiety, and fear.

I had finally come home.

CHAPTER 1

Growing Up Different

India is a wonderful country, yet I wasn't destined to live there. Although my parents are ethnically Indian, originating from Hyderabad Sindh, I was born in the beautiful country of Singapore.

My paternal grandfather was a textile merchant who owned a family business in Sri Lanka, importing and exporting European, Indian, and Chinese textiles throughout the world. Because of the nature of our company, my father was required to travel around before finally settling down in what was the British colony of Hong Kong when I was just two years old.

My origins immersed me in three cultures and languages simultaneously. Hong Kong, a vibrant and bustling metropolis, is a city predominantly populated by Chinese, so I learned to speak Cantonese with the local people. My parents sent both my brother, Anoop, and me to British schools, where the teaching was in English, and most of my schoolmates were British expatriates. At home, however, my family spoke our native Sindhi language and practiced the Hindu way of life.

My father was a tall, handsome man, who commanded respect from his family. Although I knew he loved us, his manner was strict, and he expected us to conform to his rules. I was afraid of him, and as a child, I made sure that I never crossed him. In contrast, my mother was always kindly toward both my brother and myself, and I never feared sharing my feelings with her.

I absolutely adored Anoop, and we've been very close our whole lives, even though he's five years older than I am. For a child, this is a substantial age gap, so we rarely played together, nor did we ever squabble. Instead, I looked up to him, and he was very protective of me. I felt very safe when he was around, and knew that I could speak to him about anything. He has always been a stronger male influence in my life than my father.

As traditional Hindus, my parents had an arranged marriage, and they hoped to someday set up suitable matches for Anoop and me when we were old enough. Also, traditionally, a woman would be required to be subservient to her husband and to the men of the household.

Such gender inequality is rife in my culture. As a young child, however, I didn't question these values and took for granted that this is the way things were supposed to be. My first uncomfortable experience with this disparity came at the tender age of six when I overheard a conversation between another lady and my mother.

"Were you disappointed that your second child was a girl when she was born?" this woman asked in our Indian dialect.

I felt a sense of anxiety rise within me as I awaited the response.

"No, of course not. I love my daughter!" my mother replied, much to my relief.

"But girls are a problem, especially when they grow up," the woman said. "With girls, you have to make sure they don't get spoiled, otherwise they won't get a good husband. And the amount of the dowry that's required to get a daughter married only gets higher with each passing year!"

"You can't predict the future. Every child, whether girl or boy, brings with them their own fate," I recall my mother replying wisely.

"Well, I'm happy that I have two sons!" the woman said proudly. Even my young mind was able to detect the sense of achievement she felt as she made that statement.

Later, when my mother and I were alone together, I asked, "Mama, is it true that girls are a problem?"

"No, of course not, *Beta* darling," she responded. (*Beta* is an affectionate term for "my child" in our dialect.)

My mother pulled me close and gave me a hug, and at that moment, I recall thinking, *I never want to be a problem to my parents just because I'm a girl. I don't want them to ever wish I were born a boy.*

OUR FIRST HOME IN HONG KONG WAS an apartment in a nine-story building in Happy Valley overlooking the horse-racing track. I used to spend hours looking out the window at the jockeys in their colorful silks, training the horses for the weekend races.

The tramline ran along the main road outside our apartment block, and the trams would noisily interrupt my daydreams as they rumbled past below me while I gazed out of our seventh-floor apartment window.

Most mornings I'd roll myself out of bed to the familiar rich fragrance of sandalwood and rose-scented incense. I've always loved the aroma, as it offered me a sense of peace and serenity. I'd usually find my mother, dressed in one of her myriad colored *salwaar kameez* (traditional Indian dress), made mostly of fine Indian silks or French chiffons, about to enter our home shrine.

Every morning, my parents meditated, prayed, and chanted mantras at our shrine in front of the deities Krishna, Laxmi, Shiva, Hanuman, and Ganesha. They did this to raise their consciousness for inner strength as they faced another day. My parents followed the scriptures contained within the Hindu Vedas, as well as the teachings of Guru Nanak and his holy book, the Guru Granth Sahib.

I often sat in front of the shrine and watched my parents intently as they lit the incense and waved it in a circular motion in front of the little statues and pictures of the various gods and goddesses, while chanting their *puja* (Hindu prayer), and I would emulate them.

Later on, I'd watch our Chinese nanny, Ah Fong, attend to her various chores as she chattered to me in Cantonese. Her tiny body, dressed in the traditional black-and-white *samfoo* (traditional Chinese dress), made quick little movements as she scurried through the house. I was very attached to Ah Fong. She'd been with us since I was two years old, and I couldn't remember a time when she wasn't part of our family.

ON A TYPICAL WEEKDAY, I WOULDN'T SEE my parents until early evening. Ah Fong would pick me up from school, and after going home for lunch, she often took me to the market to purchase fresh food and produce for our household. We traveled by tram, and I used to delight in going with her on those outings.

We hopped onto the tram as it stopped on the street right outside my apartment building. It was such an adventure for me. I gazed out the window as the tram made its way through the crowded, narrow streets of Hong Kong; through Happy Valley, Causeway Bay, and Wan Chai; and then we got off at the market, Ah Fong gripping my little hand tightly. I delighted in taking in all the sights, smells, and sounds of my surroundings. My parents never took me to such exciting places! They only traveled by car and shopped in department stores, which I thought was dull in comparison to this kaleidoscope of color and sensation.

The markets sold everything, from fresh produce and household goods to trinkets and baubles. The vendors called out their wares, and the stalls were in no special order. Vegetable stalls were interspersed with stalls selling shoes, flowers, pots and pans, cheap plastic toys, colorful arrays of fresh fruit, costume jewelry, balloons, fresh fish, meat, socks and stockings, colorful napkins and towels, tablecloths, and so on, most of them with the wares spilling out onto the street. I was mesmerized for hours.

"Ah Fong, Ah Fong! Look at that! What's that man doing with the snake?" I cried out excitedly in my fluent Cantonese.

"That's a snake vendor. He's going to tie up that snake, and that family is going to take it home to make snake soup," Ah Fong replied.

I continued to watch in wide-eyed wonder as the snake writhed to fight for its freedom in the skillful hands of its handler—but to no avail. I felt compassion for the poor creature as it was expertly tied up with bamboo strips and caged in wire meshing.

Nevertheless, I absolutely loved going to the markets with Ah Fong. These little outings were a field day for my strong sense of adventure!

EVEN AFTER MANY YEARS OF LIVING WITH US, Ah Fong still lowered her eyes and averted her gaze each time my mother or father entered the room. Being an inquisitive child, I flooded her with questions about everything, including her behavior. In my mind, I was always trying to reconcile the cultural differences between Ah Fong and my parents.

"How come you do that?" my six-year-old self wanted to know.

"How come I do what?" Ah Fong replied

"How come you look down when my parents come near you?" I asked in Cantonese.

"To show respect," she explained

"How come?"

"Your parents are my employers. I want to show I respect them and realize that they are my superiors."

"Are they your superiors?" I was amazed by this piece of information.

"Yes, because they give me work."

"Am *I* your superior?" I asked

Ah Fong laughed good-naturedly, as she was used to my persistently inquiring mind.

"No, you didn't give me work. I'm here to look after you."

"Oh, okay," I called back as I left to play with my new doll.

I also loved playing with Ah Fong's daughter, Ah Moh Yee. From the time I was about five years old, Ah Moh Yee came to stay with her mother at our home on the weekends. She was only a year older than I, and because I spoke fluent Cantonese, we became friends. I really enjoyed her company. We played together with my toys, and we also went to the nearby park together. My parents were very happy for me to have a live-in playmate every weekend.

Sunday being Ah Fong's day off, she took Ah Mo Yee out for lunch and then dropped her daughter back at her own parents' home, where she lived during the week. (Although I never questioned it at the time, looking back, I realize that Ah Fong was a single mother, bringing up Ah Mo Yee with the help of her family.) Ah Fong took me with her if I wasn't going out with my parents, and I really cherished those outings.

As usual, we traveled everywhere by tram, beginning by going to a Chinese food stall for a meal. These places, called *dai pai dong* in Cantonese, were outdoors on the street, so we sat on little wooden stools, slurping bowls of hot noodles and dumplings in soup while traffic drove past. After the meal, Ah Fong took us to the home where Ah Mo Yee lived with her grandparents, a modest and sparsely furnished low-rise Chinese-style walk-up loft apartment. I made my way around the dark, stone interior of the apartment, my curious mind wanting to explore every corner, as Ah Fong sipped tea with her parents. They drank tea out of little cups with colorful enamel designs of the animals from the Chinese zodiac, such as dragons or tigers, while I had a glass tumbler filled with juice or sweet tea.

I never got bored of going there, and even if I tired of the conversation, I enjoyed looking out of the large arched windows at the street below, where the dried-seafood vendors laid out fresh scallops and fish onto straw matting to dry out on the side of the road in the strong afternoon sun.

THUS, MY CHILDHOOD WAS A MIXTURE of East and West. Since Hong Kong was a British colony mainly inhabited by Chinese, Christmas and Easter were celebrated with the same enthusiasm as the Hungry Ghost and Mid-Autumn Moon Festivals.

Ah Fong and Ah Mo Yee taught me about Chinese traditions and beliefs, as well as the meaning behind all the festivals, and I loved the fact that Ah Mo Yee stayed with us during all her holidays. For example, the Hungry Ghost Festival was held on the 14th night of the seventh month of the lunar calendar. During that day, families prayed for the pains of their deceased relatives and gave offerings to their ancestors who had died.

Anoop and I watched Ah Fong and Ah Mo Yee, as well as Ah Chun, the cook, make offerings to their deceased relatives by burning effigies of fine goods made of paper. They lit a fire inside a large urn at the back of our home, at the bottom of the stairwell behind the kitchen, and fed the paper to the fire. The effigies resembled cars, houses, and even fake money. It was anticipated that their ancestors were receiving these luxuries in the other realm.

"Ah Fong, does your grandpa really receive a house in heaven if you burn that paper house?" I asked curiously.

"Yes, Anita. My grandparents expect me to continue to remember them and support them, even in the afterlife. We all have to respect our ancestors," she told me.

Ah Fong, Ah Chun, and Ah Mo Yee then sat down to a meal at their table at the back of the kitchen, which Ah Chun had spent a fair part of the day preparing, with an extra place set at the table for the deceased relatives to join in the festivities. There were offerings of food in front of the extra place set for the departed. I often joined them for this meal, and showed genuine concern about whether the ancestors were getting enough food put in front of them!

One of my favorite times of the year was the Mid-Autumn Moon Festival, which was when I got to choose a brilliantly colorful paper lantern from the myriad on display, hanging from the ceilings of many local stores. The lanterns came in all shapes and sizes, including the animals of the Chinese zodiac. I always loved the rabbit shape best! Ah Fong took both Ah Mo Yee and me to choose our lanterns together from the shops behind the markets.

In some ways, this festival is very similar to the American holiday Thanksgiving, and it's the celebration of the large harvest moon. The ceremony includes eating and distributing moon cakes, of which there are numerous varieties. We then lit the candles inside the beautiful and colorful paper lanterns and took them outside. Together with the other children in our neighborhood, Ah Mo Yee and I hung our lanterns outside our homes, and on trees and fences. We were allowed to stay up later than usual on this night and play by the light of the lanterns and the moon, which was at its fullest and brightest for the year.

MY FAMILY ALSO CELEBRATED ALL THE INDIAN FESTIVALS, including Diwali (the Hindu Festival of Lights), with great enthusiasm. We always wore new clothes for the occasion, and it was a very exciting time for me. Even at that young age, I absolutely loved the idea of shopping for a new outfit prior to the festivities! My mother usually took my brother and me to Lane Crawford, at that time the largest department store in the central business district of Hong Kong. We ran up and down the children's department, me looking excitedly at the dresses and pinafores, my brother looking at the shirts and trousers. My mother would help me pick out a dress, and for this time of year, it was usually the more colorful the better, to go with the festive occasion.

On the auspicious evening, my whole family got all dressed up in our new clothes, my mother usually in a brand-new, colorful sari, wearing all her jewelry; my father in a traditional *kurta patloon* (Indian shirt and pants); my brother in trousers and a shirt; and me in a new dress.

After getting all dressed up, we went to the Hindu temple in Happy Valley to mingle with others from our Indian community and sing *bhajans*, which are Hindu devotional songs.

Our voices, interspersed with chimes and bells, echoed through the high, domed ceiling of the temple and drifted out into the evening air. I remember actually feeling the sounds of the temple bells reverberate through my very being, touching a deep part of my soul. On every Hindu festival day, the temple courtyard came alive with color, music, dance, and the smells of spicy Indian vegetarian food weaving their way amidst the sweet fragrance of incense. How I loved the atmosphere!

"Mama, I'm going to the front, to get the *mahraj* [Indian priest] to put vermillion on my forehead!" I cried out to my mother excitedly in Sindhi, as my small body wove its way through the colorful crowd.

The vermillion streak that the mahraj dabs on each person's forehead signifies the opening of the third eye, and I always ensured that I got my red streak each time I went to the temple.

Because of my Hindu roots, I grew up to believe in karma and reincarnation. Most Eastern religions are based on these laws, believing that the purpose of life is to raise our consciousness and spiritually evolve through each cycle of birth and death to the point of reaching enlightenment. At that point, we break the cycle of birth and death and no longer need to reincarnate into a flesh-and-blood body. That state is called *nirvana*.

Thinking about this sometimes made me anxious, so I was careful not to do anything that could possibly create negative karma in a future life. Even as a youngster, my mind continuously processed what could be construed as creating good karma versus bad, as I tried to perfect myself against a barometer created by my cultural beliefs.

My Hindu religion also taught me that meditation and chanting are two of many methods commonly used to cleanse the mind of impure thoughts and assist us in our quest for enlightenment. Meditation helps us develop the awareness that we're much more than our physical selves. So as I grew older, I was already aware that we're more than our biology.

CHAPTER 2

Many Religions, Many Paths

In contrast to the Hindu traditions I learned at home, my early education began at a Catholic school run by nuns. And by the time I was seven, I'd already started to learn the impact of cultural and religious differences. The school was housed in a beautiful, expansive old building that was three stories high and crowned with a lovely domed chapel. The school also happened to be conveniently located within short walking distance of our home.

On my first day, I wore my new uniform with great pride. It consisted of a crisp white pinafore and a navy-blue blazer with a smart red emblem on it. I felt really good about myself because when I entered the school grounds, I saw all the other children dressed the same way I was. The uniform gave me a sense of belonging. We started each day by singing hymns, which I also thoroughly enjoyed.

"How come your family doesn't go to church on Sundays?" my classmate Joseph wanted to know one day, after I'd been attending school for about a month.

"Because we aren't Catholic. We're Hindu and we go to the temple on Monday evenings," I said.

"You need to tell your parents to take you to church to pray to God every Sunday, otherwise you won't get to heaven when you die," Joseph told me.

"Are you sure about that?" I asked. "Because if it were true, I'm sure my parents would know."

"Of course I'm sure—just ask any of the others in school. Or even better, ask Sister Mary at our next Bible-study class. She knows the truth for sure. She knows what God really wants!" he persisted.

I liked Joseph. He seemed to care and really wanted me to go to heaven. So I took my question to Sister Mary, and needless to say, she reiterated my need to go to church and study the Bible if I wanted to win God's favor. She kindly offered to help me understand the words of God.

That afternoon when I got home from school, I decided to talk to my mother about what Sister Mary had said.

"Mama, my friends and the Sisters at my school say that I have to go to church on Sundays, and I have to study the Bible if I want to go to heaven when I die."

"No, Beta," my mother said. "You don't have to worry about that. Just tell everyone at school that we're Hindus; and when you're a little older, you'll study *our* scriptures, the Vedas. People from different places have different faiths. You'll come to learn that after we die, we're reincarnated into other circumstances."

"I don't think the kids in my school are going to buy that," I said somewhat sullenly. "And I'm scared. What if they're right? They can't all be wrong. How can the Sisters be wrong?"

My mother pulled me close and said, "Don't be scared, Beta. No one really knows the truth—not even Sister Mary. Religion is just a path for finding truth: Religion is not *truth*. It is just a *path*. And different people follow different paths."

ALTHOUGH TEMPORARILY COMFORTING, MY MOTHER'S WORDS didn't completely alleviate my ongoing fears. Over time, my apprehension over not conforming to the religion of my peers grew worse rather than better.

I wanted Sister Mary to tell me that I could still get to heaven even though I was Hindu, but she wouldn't give me the assurance I was looking for. From what I'd learned at school, I understood the grim fate that awaited those who didn't make it.

What if God decides to come for me while I'm sleeping? Sister Mary said that he's everywhere and knows everything. That means he knows I haven't been baptized!

So I lay awake at night, not daring to sleep in case God took that opportunity to show me the fate that awaited those who weren't in his favor.

My parents became more concerned by my anxiety and my sleepless nights. When they realized that my fears were getting worse and not better with time, they decided to have me transferred at the age of eight to the Island School.

Just a little cluster of six buildings and surrounding grounds, this British school was nestled in the hills of Hong Kong just above Bowen Road. It was more secular, and at that time, the students were mainly the children of British expatriates who either ran the government or worked in the multinational corporations that helped to build and develop our city.

The school itself was lavish, beautiful, and state of the art for its time, with science and language labs, an experimental zoo, gymnasiums, and swimming pools. However, as an Indian child in a predominantly British environment, I continued to struggle. Most of the other kids in my class were blond with blue eyes, so I was often singled out and picked on just for being darker skinned and having thick, dark, wavy hair.

My mind was filled with thoughts such as, *I wish Billy would stop calling me names like "Sambo"!* In addition, I tended to be the last to be chosen for teams and was rarely asked to join in and play games. The other kids also took my things when I wasn't looking, such as my books and pens.

Such behavior made me feel lonely, sad, and dejected, but I held back my tears in public and cried into my pillow when I was alone in my bedroom at home. I didn't even want my parents to know that I was being bullied because I didn't want them to think of me as a problem. After all, they'd already made me change schools once, so I kept pretending that I was adjusting well and was really happy.

Even so, one specific incident had a strong impact on me. I was sitting in the canteen, minding my own business and eating my lunch, when Billy, who'd just finished, got up from his seat diagonally across from me. He picked up his tray of leftovers, and as he walked past me, deliberately spilled the trash on his tray straight into my lunch.

Everyone sitting around me burst into peals of laughter. It may have been only a handful of people who noticed what Billy had just done, but it felt as though everyone in the room was laughing at me.

I felt a huge rage rise up within me. I'd reached the point where I'd had enough. I was sick of being called Sambo, being the last to be chosen for teams, being picked on, and having my belongings taken from me. I just couldn't take it anymore.

I stood up with a jolt, picked up my cup of sweet orange soda, and turned around to face Billy, who was now also looking at me and laughing. I looked at him square in the face, and poured the drink over his head!

Now the entire room did burst out laughing, but thankfully, this time it wasn't at me. They were looking at Billy, standing there with sticky orange soda dripping down from his hair and running all down his face and clothes. He looked a real sight, but I was too scared to laugh. I was afraid of his reaction.

Billy glared at me with so much anger in his eyes that I felt as though they were boring holes right through me, and I didn't stick around long enough to see any more of his reaction. I ran. I bolted out of the canteen like lightning, went into the girls' washroom, locked myself inside a toilet cubicle, and started to cry. I cried because I knew what I'd done was out of character for me. I wanted more than anything to fit in, to be accepted and liked. I couldn't change my skin color or race, and it made me feel so helpless!

Why am I always different, wherever I go? Where do I belong? Why don't I feel like I belong anywhere? I desperately wanted to know as I let out deep sobs, crouched inside the small cubicle.

THANKFULLY, AS I GOT OLDER AND entered into my teen years, the bullying eventually subsided. However, as my classmates started to gain independence, I found my parents becoming stricter, particularly when it came to going out in the evenings with my friends, and especially if boys were involved. Going out with boys was frowned upon in our culture, so I was rarely able to attend our school youth evenings or go out on the weekends with my classmates.

As a result, I never felt that I belonged. I always felt left out when my classmates talked about their weekend evenings at the youth dances, laughing and sharing stories. I watched them with envy, and so wished that I wasn't Indian. I was left to focus on my academic studies instead and kept to myself most of the time. I spent countless hours locked inside my own world, and I had very few friends whom I was really close to.

My parents continued to try their utmost to indoctrinate me into our own culture and to have me meet other Indian people, but I pushed back against their attempts.

"I don't want to go to *Vedanta* class," I proclaimed to my mother one Saturday when I was about 13. Vedanta is the study of Hindu scriptures, and I used to attend weekly lessons where I met other Indian children.

"Then things will be more difficult for you as you grow up, particularly when you get married. You need to know what it means to be Hindu," my mother told me as she fussed with my hair.

But I don't want to be more Indian! I want to be more like my classmates! I thought. Aloud, I told her, "But I want to go out with my other friends—my friends from school. They don't have to attend Vedanta class!"

"Your father and I want you to attend, and that is all there is to it," she said.

I still wasn't convinced that I wanted to be a Hindu, but as a good Indian girl, I obeyed my parents' wishes. Over many years, my Indian friends and I met at our classes every week to learn the ins and outs of our faith. I found the Vedic teachings in and of themselves to be interesting and stimulating to study. We had a great teacher who encouraged discussion, which I was very good at. I was a popular member of the class, which was in sharp contrast to how I felt at school, where I so desperately wanted to fit in. I felt as though I were leading two separate lives.

How I wish I could merge everything and be as popular at school as I am with my Indian friends, I often thought. *Why can't my schoolmates see in me what my Indian friends see?*

As I got older, I became more and more interested in the intellectual aspects of the study of Hinduism. I actually enjoyed studying the Bhagavad Gita and the Vedas, learning about cause and effect, destiny versus free will, and similar topics; and I loved the discourses and debates we had on these subjects. Also, I prayed and meditated, because I felt it cleared my thoughts at that time. There was much about it that actually made sense to me, even though many of the beliefs of my culture didn't seem rational, such as suppressing women, expecting them to be subservient to men, and arranging marriages against people's will. Nowhere is any of this stipulated in the Vedas!

Despite my exposure to such a broad range of cultures and religions, nothing prepared me for what would transpire in the years to come. Little did I know that all my previously held beliefs, perceptions, and philosophies were going to be blown wide open and shaken to their very core. Long before that, however, I was still challenging my culture and traditions as I moved into adulthood and searched for balance in my life.

CHAPTER 3

Matchmaking Missteps

Over the years, because of our culture, my parents tried to gently persuade me toward an arranged marriage by introducing me to the sons of friends and acquaintances. My father in particular wasn't keen on my furthering my studies beyond high school, as he feared my going away from home to college would make me more independent. He believed that this would reduce my chances of being a subservient and accommodating housewife one day. In my culture, it's believed that the less educated and younger a woman is, the more accommodating she'll be in a marriage, which is considered desirable.

Although my parents wanted nothing more in the world than for me to be happy, in their minds, this hinged not only on me getting married, but specifically marrying someone from my own culture. However, everything I wanted to do seemed to contradict this.

"But Dad, I really want to go to university to study photography and graphic design!" I insisted.

"If you can find a course of study near home, I won't object, but I'm not letting you live away from home to study!" my father responded.

"But Dad, you know that there are no higher education institutes that teach in English around here! I have to move away if I want to study further!" I argued.

"That's out of the question! You know very well that it is not acceptable for women to live away from home before they're married," he countered.

But I'd grown into a young woman by this point, with my own strong views and opinions. Because of my education, I'd become much more westernized in my outlook, so I asked, "Why are the rules different for women then they are for men?"

"They aren't rules! They're just the way things are, and you should be proud of upholding your cultural values," my father said, somewhat annoyed by my defiance.

I had dreams that I had yet to fulfill, and I had a sinking feeling they might not come to fruition. I wanted to see the world and maybe work as a travel photographer. I wanted to backpack through Europe, see the Eiffel Tower in Paris, and experience the pyramids of Egypt. I wanted to feel the energy of Machu Picchu, eat paella in Spain, and enjoy tagine in Morocco. There was so much I wanted to do, see, and experience; and I knew that agreeing to an arranged marriage would end my chances of realizing my dreams. However, my case wasn't helped by the fact that two of my closest Indian girlfriends were engaged to be married in arranged alliances at that time, shortly after graduating from high school.

So, not wanting to cause trouble or confront my father any further, I enrolled in a local photography course. At the same time, I humored my parents and played the role of demure prospective bride when they asked me to meet suitable matches.

I RECALL ON ONE PARTICULAR OCCASION, my parents asked me to dress in my best traditional clothes as they accompanied me to meet another prospective groom. I wore a deep pink raw-silk top with delicate embroidery around its broad neckline. I had a fine, pastel pink lace shawl with matching embroidered trim loosely draped over my head and shoulders in order to project an air of modesty. This outfit was completed with silk pants in pastel blue, and a pair of pale pink stiletto pumps.

I remember clearly that during the entire car ride, I was mentally constructing a checklist of definite conversational no-nos in this situation. I found myself thinking that I mustn't let slip that I was much more comfortable in jeans and sneakers or hiking boots than in traditional Indian clothes. And another faux pas would be admitting that unlike in my earlier years, I rarely visited the Hindu temple for weekly prayers, except maybe during festivals. I knew that I must also refrain from talking about my hobbies and other interests—my affinity for eclectic music; my love of art, astronomy, and stargazing; and my passion for being out in nature. I decided that I shouldn't talk about any of my aspirations for the future, of someday biking across Africa, backpacking through Europe, visiting Egypt, being a social activist involved with organizations that build self-sustaining and environmentally friendly global villages in developing countries, or working to improve the prospects for people in some of the poverty-stricken nations in Asia.

No, I told myself, *I must remember not to bring up any of that.*

I recall making a mental note to specifically mention, in the presence of my prospective mother-in-law, my recently acquired skill of rolling a perfect *chapatti*. This traditional unleavened bread is a staple in most Indian households, and requires great skill to roll evenly so that the dough forms in a perfect circle. I knew that would please the family sufficiently.

I really thought I had it all worked out. I believed I'd thought through all the possible scenarios this time and that nothing could go wrong. But it turned out that I hadn't done my homework properly. When we got to the venue, a lovely colonial club nestled in the hillside of Old Peak Road, the waiter came around to take everyone's orders. I asked for a tuna sandwich, not realizing that the prospective groom and his family were all strict vegetarians. It didn't even occur to me as each member of the family ordered either a cheese-and-cucumber sandwich, a cheese-and-onion pie, or some other vegetarian option.

The words "I'll have a tuna sandwich" had barely left my lips when the prospective groom's mother shot a look at me that felt as though it were boring through the core of my being. In unison, the rest of the family followed her gaze. As all eyes fell on me, I just sat there, wishing that the floor would open up and swallow me.

I felt so stupid for my mistake! *How could I not have noticed—or even considered—that they could be vegetarian?* I chastised myself over and over again. After all, it's not something that's uncommon in my culture.

Needless to say, that particular arrangement didn't go further than the first meeting.

At one point, however, one of the matchmaking efforts *did* lead to an engagement. After only meeting twice, the young man and I had to make a decision as to whether we wanted to get engaged before we could see each other again.

We weren't allowed to spend more time together until we decided how we wanted to move forward. He was tall, handsome, and well spoken. I was attracted to him and could tell that he felt the same way about me. We were interested in getting to know each other better, so much to the delight of our parents, we agreed to make the commitment. This took place in the form of a religious ceremony at the Guru Nanak temple, attended by all our family and friends and blessed by the mahraj. This event is called the *misri*, and can loosely be translated as an engagement ceremony.

Our misri took place in the afternoon and was followed that evening by a dinner party at a well-established Indian restaurant. The food and wine flowed, there was music, and we danced for the very first time. In that moment, I was gloriously happy. I finally felt that I was doing the right thing, that I was going to be accepted by one and all. I believed that I was about to live happily ever after.

Unfortunately, over the months, as it got closer to the wedding date, I started to realize that I'd never be the person my fiancé and his family wanted for a wife and daughter-in-law, because I didn't fit the traditional mold. How could I not have realized this before making the commitment? The fact that it was an arranged marriage should have alerted me to the fact that it came with certain expectations. Yet since the arrangement had been solidified, breaking it off seemed out of the question, at least as far as the two families were concerned.

During the time this man and I were engaged, I kept hoping that I could change for him and his family. I struggled to become someone whom they'd be proud to call their wife and daughter-in-law. But regrettably, I only continued to disappoint them and fall short of their expectations. I desperately wanted to please them, but I found it hard to stay focused on my traditional duties because of my restlessness and desire to follow my dreams.

I felt so disappointed in myself during this time. I kept wondering, *Why is this so difficult for me? What's wrong with me? Others do it so easily. People are getting engaged and married all the time, including all of my own friends! Why am I struggling so much with the idea?* I felt powerless and worthless. I felt like such a failure.

Finally, I submitted to the fact that I might never be the kind of person they were looking for. I was ready to admit defeat because I knew I couldn't go through with it any longer.

I was so scared—scared to tell anyone, and of the reaction I was going to get if I did. I was scared of getting married and of breaking it off.

Deep down, I knew that I'd never meet the expectations of my future husband or my in-laws. Everything I'd been doing up to that point—the way I'd been dressing and behaving—it was all an act. I knew I'd never truly be what they wanted me to be. I'd end up spending my entire life trying to be someone I wasn't, and I'd always fall short. I'd also never get a chance to realize any of my own dreams, hopes, and wishes.

During all this, I hadn't told my parents any of what I'd been feeling or how much I'd been struggling, because once again, I didn't want them to think of me as a problem. I'd kept everything to myself and put on a brave front, appearing to be happy and always smiling and laughing readily, going through all the motions that a happily engaged young woman would. I hadn't shared this information with anyone, because I didn't want to burden others with my emotional pains and fears.

But I'd reached the point where I couldn't hold it together anymore, so one evening shortly before the wedding day, I went to my mother and burst into tears.

"Mum, I'm so sorry!" I cried. "I can't do it! I just can't do it!

To my surprise, my mother hugged me and said, "Don't cry, darling. Just tell me everything that's troubling you."

"I'm not ready, Mum! I have dreams, and I want to travel the world and do different things, and I just can't bear the thought that I'm not going to ever have the independence again to do all the things I want to do!"

I blurted out everything that I was feeling between deep sobs. I let out all my thoughts and fears, all my dreams, hopes, and aspirations.

My mother held me close and told me that she wasn't going to force me to go through with anything I didn't want to do. She apologized to me for not recognizing my fears earlier, and also for her part in making me undergo all this, at least thus far. She said that she needed to talk to my father, but she told me not to be afraid and that she'd support me through my decision.

I felt a cathartic release that I'd never felt before.

Then I spoke to Anoop about everything I'd told my mother. He immediately said, "Don't worry, sis, I'm here for you. I wish you'd shared your feelings with us earlier. You needn't have struggled with your emotions alone."

"But I didn't realize I had a choice after the engagement," I remember telling him tearfully.

However, other than my immediate family, no one in our community took the news well at all.

RELATIVES, FAMILY MEMBERS, PROSPECTIVE family members, and others in our community were saddened, angry, and disappointed to hear this news. They came to see me, attempting to persuade me to go through with the wedding. They told me that it was normal to feel the way I did, that everything would be fine afterward, and that I should go through with it anyway. They tried to convince me that if I broke my commitment, no one else in our culture would want to marry me. My name would be tarnished, and no family would let their son near me.

They tried to convince me that my ideals were unrealistic, especially for a woman. My expectations were too high, and I'd never find a suitable man because of this. Lower your expectations, be an obedient wife and daughter-in-law, and you'll have a good life, I was told.

I felt absolutely terrible for hurting everyone as I stood my ground. When I heard what people were beginning to say about me, I felt terrible about my decision and afraid for my future. People said that I wasn't domesticated enough, that I was spoiled, and that my parents hadn't brought me up properly. They also said that to be able to do something like that as a woman, I had too high an opinion of myself. I felt awful and sad. I didn't want to socialize within our culture anymore. I regretted everything I'd done, from getting engaged to breaking off the engagement, for hurting my fiancé and his family, for hurting my family, for not being domesticated enough, for not being Indian enough. In fact, I regretted everything about myself.

Why am I always apologizing? Why do I have to apologize just for being me? I just couldn't understand what was wrong with me.

I couldn't bear all the explaining I had to do and the people I had to deal with. So just days before the wedding was to take place, with everything bought and paid for—all the arrangements made, gifts piling up, and friends and relatives arriving from different parts of the world—I ran away. I went on a long trip to see some of my old friends in India and the UK. I just wanted to disappear, to get out of the way of our community until everything simmered down, because I didn't want to deal with anything except my own emotions. I needed to sort myself out. I knew that the next phase of my life wasn't going to be easy.

CHAPTER 4

My True Love

After I returned to my parents' home in Hong Kong, I didn't want to integrate back into the Indian community since I felt like a complete social misfit. So I turned my attention toward developing a career in an attempt to gain some independence.

"I got the job!" I cried one day as I burst through the front door of our apartment, where my father was sitting in his favorite armchair, watching the evening news.

One of my friends had told me about a vacancy where she worked, because she thought the job would be a perfect fit for me. Her employer was a French fashion-accessory company that distributed their goods throughout Asia. The position would entail assisting the sales manager in promoting the products and fulfilling wholesale orders, with the possibility of travel to neighboring cities. I wasn't normally attracted to sales and distribution, but was excited mainly because of the potential for travel and independence.

"Well done, Beta! I knew you would get it!" My father beamed proudly as he turned to face me. "Tell me all about it. When do you start? Who do you report to? What are your responsibilities?"

"I start on the first of next month. I'm so excited! I'll be reporting to the regional export manager. The position holds great future potential. If I can prove myself to my boss and help him exceed his targets, they'll give me some territories to handle independently."

"What does that mean?" my father asked, now looking a little less enthusiastic.

"It means that there's a huge possibility that I may get to travel all around the region!"

"Although I'm really proud of you, darling," my father said, "I want you to remember that this is only something to pass the time until you find a husband. I don't want you to be so involved in your career that you become too independent to get married! Your mother and I are still hoping to find the perfect match for you."

"Aw, Dad—don't spoil my moment! I'm really excited about this position!"

"Yes, I know," he said. "Well, you never can tell, these days some husbands don't mind their wives having jobs. I just don't want you to get disappointed later if your future husband doesn't approve of your work and travel, that's all. But you're right—let's not think of the future right now. Today, let's celebrate your success!"

"Where's Mum? I want to tell her the good news. Then I want to take you both out for dinner—my treat!" I called out as I left the room to phone Anoop and share my good news with him.

At last things were starting to work out for me. I was beginning to gain independence both financially and socially.

OVER THE YEARS, ALTHOUGH MY PARENTS continued attempting to arrange matches for me, they slowly began to realize that they were fighting a losing battle.

Their attempts frustrated me somewhat because they still didn't understand that within the confines of our culture, I wasn't considered typical; and my reputation was tarnished because of the broken engagement. I was aware that people from my culture thought of me as strong-minded, rebellious, idealistic, stubborn, and opinionated—all of which were not desirable traits for a woman. Despite all this, my parents continued to hold out hope that if they introduced me to the right man, I'd change for him and become more domesticated.

In the meantime, my career at the French company had taken off, and my position required me to visit neighboring cities. Although still living at home with my parents when I was in Hong Kong, the traveling allowed me a level of freedom and independence that I enjoyed and appreciated, and it gave me the opportunity to meet all kinds of people from all walks of life. Slowly, I started to feel good about life again. In fact, I felt happy, popular, and successful, when I was *outside the confines of my culture*. I loved this side of my life—the people in it, my work, and the travel involved. The role of a traditional Indian housewife held no appeal for me at all. That was the furthest thing from my mind, and I could see no benefit to giving up what I had, so I continued to dissuade my parents' attempts at finding the perfect mate for me.

But in the back of my mind, I always carried the feeling of being inadequate in some way. I felt that I'd failed or not achieved the standard expected of me. This nagging voice followed me everywhere, making sure that I never felt quite good enough or deserving enough. I was somehow damaged goods . . . or *flawed* . . .

ONE DAY IN LATE 1992, QUITE UNEXPECTEDLY, I met the man who'd eventually become my husband, although at first I didn't believe that he was the perfect man for me. We met by chance one evening through someone with whom we were both acquainted.

"Do you know a guy by the name of Danny Moorjani?" Naina asked me over the phone as I sat at my desk at work, trying to complete the weekly sales report to meet the weekend deadline. Naina was a friend who didn't live in Hong Kong but was visiting at the time, and we were going out for a drink after work that evening.

"No, I've never met him." I answered. "Why do you ask, and who is he?"

"He's a really cute Sindhi guy I met while I was in New York last summer. Apparently he lives and works in Hong Kong. I'm surprised you've never met him," she answered.

"You know me. I shy away from our community, particularly after the 'incident'! There are a lot of Sindhi people in Hong Kong I've never met, so it's hardly surprising," I responded.

"Well, you're about to meet him," she said. "I tracked him down and asked him to join us for drinks this evening."

Later that night, when Naina and I walked into Club '97, a sophisticated bar and lounge in the heart of the city, I identified this man immediately, although I'd never met him before. There he was, standing casually by himself, dressed in a maroon turtle-necked sweater and black trousers. He looked over as we came through the entrance, and although he was there to meet Naina, I noticed that his gaze was following my every move as we walked toward him and sat down. Even as my friend greeted him, I saw that he didn't look away from me, and the moment his eyes met mine, a feeling of recognition seemed to burst through each of us. It felt as though we'd known each other forever, and the sensation was electrifying. I was well aware that he was feeling exactly the same way, and we started talking.

We connected on so many levels, and by the end of the evening, we'd exchanged phone numbers. To my excitement, he called me the very next day, and we went out for dinner together. He was incredibly romantic, bringing me flowers and taking me to a lovely restaurant, Jimmy's Kitchen, which is still one of our favorites today.

However, the more we were connecting over the weeks, the more I found myself pulling away, because I didn't trust my instincts. Being with him was both quixotic and electrifying, and I hadn't felt that way in a very long time. It scared me. I was afraid because he was Sindhi. I didn't want to get involved with a man from my own culture, at least not now . . . maybe not ever.

I knew very well that marrying within the Indian culture usually meant an alliance with the entire family. It wouldn't be two people tying the knot, but two families. I was afraid to get involved once more in something that I'd regret. I wanted to marry the man, not all his relatives, and because I knew our culture, I was afraid. I was terrified about what his family would think of me. Would it be the same situation all over again? Did his family know about my past? Would they reject me if they knew I had a broken engagement? And how could I possibly be sure that he didn't have expectations of me similar to those that most men from my culture have of their wives? I didn't want to get hurt again, nor did I want to harm anyone else.

But Danny was very patient and gave me all the time I needed, and I appreciated that about him. I found his presence irresistible, and he made me feel loved in a way I never had before. I was experiencing a battle between my heart and my mind, and my heart was winning.

As we got to know each other, I began to realize that Danny was a lot like me. He didn't relate to our culture either, since he'd also grown up in Hong Kong and been educated in the British school system. He rejected many of our customs, especially the ideas around women and marriage. He was always very generous and open in his affection for me, and his love felt genuine and unconditional. For the first time, I never felt any pressure that I had to be a certain way to win a man or that he had an agenda.

Danny also had an incredible sense of humor, and I found that very attractive. He laughed easily, and his laughter was infectious, so our dates together were always a lot of fun. He seemed to know exactly when to call and what to say at the right time. He was gentle, yet strong and persuasive, and I loved that about him.

However, I still found myself thinking that it was only a matter of time before he discovered the inherent flaws within me. I was afraid he'd soon become disappointed.

But that day never arrived. Danny was steady and unwavering in his affection for me. He called me on the phone just to see how I was doing and sent me flowers and gifts on special occasions. Unlike many of his counterparts, he loved my independent nature. And instead of being horrified by my interests, dreams, and aspirations, he found humor in my warding off my parents' attempts at arranging a marriage. He thought all these qualities of mine were endearing. He was genuinely interested in me for who I was, and this feeling of acceptance was so new and refreshing for me.

Danny had graduated from university with a business degree. As commonly happens in our culture, his father owned a company and Danny, being the only son and heir, was obligated to join the family business.

At the time, my job entailed some travel outside of Hong Kong. Since Danny's business did, too, I'd occasionally find his smiling face staring at me in various ports of call, as he purposely coordinated his trips to coincide with mine.

One evening, as we were walking along Deep Water Bay, one of my favorite beaches on Hong Kong Island, I casually asked Danny if he knew about my past engagement and what people in our community had been saying about me. We'd never spoken about it, so I was almost afraid to ask. I wasn't sure how he would feel if he hadn't already heard.

"Yes," he replied, "I've known about this almost since the time I met you. And thanks to our wonderful community, I'll even bet the version I've heard has been embellished tenfold, with lots of seasoning added for effect!"

"How did you feel about me when you found out?" I asked, a little bit concerned about what he was going to say.

"Are you sure you're ready to know the truth?" he responded, a slight smile appearing at the corners of his lips.

"Yes, the unadulterated truth, please. I can handle it," I said, bracing myself for what was coming.

"Well, when I heard about what you did, the first thing that came to my mind was: *Yes! That's just the type of woman I'd want to marry—someone who has a mind of her own!*"

A broad smile spread across my face as I felt a huge flood of relief pour over me. I remember saying, "So I take it you aren't attracted to me for my chapatti-making skills, then?"

"Hey, you underestimate my abilities, young lady! I roll a pretty mean chapatti myself—but that's not all. I do windows, bathrooms, and laundry as well!"

And at that moment, my smile broke into full-blown laughter. We both fell down on the sand and laughed until tears streamed down our cheeks. We laughed about everything and nothing at the same time.

As our laughter died down, he clambered up on his knees while I was still sitting on the sand, and our eyes met. He took both my hands in his and said, "Anita, I've been wanting to ask this from the day we met. Will you marry me?"

It was at that moment I knew. I knew for sure that he was the one for me. I had found my soul mate.

ON MARCH 17, 1995, EXACTLY TWO MONTHS after Danny proposed to me, the unexpected happened. The telephone rang as I rolled over in bed to look at the time.

What's going on? I wondered as I lifted the receiver, *It's only 5:15 in the morning.* Before I answered the phone, I knew that it wasn't good news.

"Beta, darling, is that you?" I hear my mother's tearful voice on the other end of the phone before I had a chance to speak.

"Yes, I'm here. What's wrong?" I felt the fear racing through me and heard it coming out in my voice. As I felt my heart skip a few beats, a part of me dreaded the news that would come at me through the piece of plastic I held in my hand. Another part was anxious to know and get the suspense over with.

"It's Dad," my mother's tearful voice told me. "He didn't wake up this morning. He went in his sleep."

When my father's health began to deteriorate some months prior, my parents went to India so that he could seek alternative therapies, such as ayurvedic treatments. I'd expected him to return in time for my wedding, with his health intact so we could dance the *bhangra* (a favorite Indian dance of celebration) together during the festivities. I couldn't believe this was happening. I frantically and tearfully packed my things, throwing whatever I could find into a suitcase as my brother made arrangements for both of us to take the next flight to Pune, India, about four hours outside of Mumbai.

My trip to India, the funeral, and that time with my family seem to come and go in blurred memories. But I won't forget the day we took my father's ashes, contained in a beautiful enameled urn, to the Indrayani River, which runs through the holy town of

Alandi, just east of Pune. We stood on the rocks overlooking the expanse of the river at the auspicious time of day when the mahraj had told us to be there. My brother opened the lid of the urn and tipped it slowly, letting the breeze carry the ashes and scatter them across the surface of the water. We watched, tears streaming down our cheeks, as the river carried the ashes away. How could we say good-bye to this wonderful man?

Dad, oh my dear Dad! I'm so sorry if I ever caused you any pain, I whispered to my father as I stood there with my hands held together in *pranam* (in prayer).

I'm getting married, and you aren't here to see me walk around the wedding fire. You lived for this day my entire life. How can you leave me now? I asked the waves as they swallowed up his ashes, while the tears flooded down my cheeks.

THE NEXT FEW MONTHS WERE BITTERSWEET, as my family and I seemed to be both mourning my father and talking about the upcoming celebration. I could tell that my mother was relieved that she had my wedding to look forward to, as it seemed to brighten what would have been a very difficult and sad time, and helping plan it gave her something to focus on.

Yet we all missed my father and felt so sad that he wouldn't be there for the one occasion that was so important to him. Seeing me get married had been like his life mission. But I consoled myself by reminding myself that he was there when I got engaged, and he was so happy for me. It was almost as though he passed on with a lighter heart.

Together with Danny's parents, we consulted the mahraj for an auspicious date for the wedding. We told him that it had to be later in the year, as my family was still grieving the loss of my father, and we weren't yet in the right frame of mind to celebrate. He consulted his holy almanac and, after taking into consideration our birth dates, informed us that December 6, 1995, was an auspicious date for us.

At the time, it seemed to be a long way away. However, the months flew by as we made arrangements, booked the venue, ordered the wedding sari, designed invitations, and worked through all the myriad chores that go with organizing an Indian wedding.

My mother threw herself into helping me plan the event in order to take her mind off her recent loss, and she took great pride in choosing my wedding sari and all the other outfits I was going to wear throughout the related occasions. She chose a stunning bronze-colored lace sari for me to wear on my wedding day itself, and a white sari with fine gold thread woven in a light design for the civil wedding.

So on December 6, 1995, I married my soul mate, Danny, in an elaborate Indian wedding with festivities that lasted almost a week! Our friends and relatives from all over the world flew to Hong Kong to attend the rituals and festivities that culminated in a reception under the stars on the lawn of the Hong Kong Country Club, which overlooks my favorite beach, Deep Water Bay, on the south side of Hong Kong Island.

One day several months prior to the date, we'd been discussing venues for the wedding, and I'd half-jokingly said, "Wouldn't it be great if we could get married on the beach where you proposed to me?"

We toyed with the idea for a few minutes, but quickly dismissed it when I thought about the frustration the female guests would face when they found their stilettos getting stuck in the sand. Then I remembered that just above the rocks toward one end of Deep Water Bay beach was the Hong Kong Country Club, with its sprawling lawns overlooking the very bay where Danny had proposed. It was at that moment that we decided it would be the perfect spot for the celebration.

It was a beautiful evening at the country club, and there was a cool breeze blowing as the *shenai* (Indian wedding music) echoed hauntingly into the night air. Danny and I walked hand in hand seven times around the fire to seal our union, as the mahraj chanted our wedding vows in Sanskrit. Danny looked handsome and princely, standing by my side in his *shervani* (regal wedding outfit), complete with turban. I was wearing the bronze lace sari my mother had picked out for me, and the end of it was draped loosely over my head, on top of the jasmine flowers woven into my hair. My hands and feet were painted with henna in a delicate paisley floral design, as is the tradition for Indian brides.

As we made our way around the fire, I kept looking across at the faces of my family members and could sense that my mother and brother were both aching for the presence of my father, wishing he were there to experience the special evening.

After the rituals were completed, a huge celebration ensued, with food, drink, music, and dancing. After the last of the functions was over, and Danny and I were in our hotel room for our wedding night, I was both exhausted and excited at the same time. I knew this was the man I wanted to be with for the rest of my life. We were going to live happily ever after . . .

CHAPTER 5

Diagnosis of Fear

As the years passed, Danny and I built our life together. He left the family business to start a career in marketing and sales for a multinational organization, and then we moved out of his bachelor pad in the heart of the city and into a lovely apartment in a quiet suburb of Hong Kong. We adopted a dog whom we named Cosmo.

Not long after I got married, my brother decided to leave Hong Kong and start up a business in India because there was a major recession in our city, and he saw an opportunity in India. So he and his wife, Mona, and their toddler son, Shahn, all moved there; and my mother followed them shortly thereafter. I missed them all terribly because I'd never lived in a different country from my family.

To make matters worse, because of the recession, I lost my job at the French company since sales had gone down dramatically. This upset me, as it came unexpectedly and added to the stress and loneliness of my family leaving Hong Kong.

During that period, I also often felt pressured by our community and my peers to have a child, although at that time, I was more interested in working, traveling, and exploring the world.

Finally, I found freelance work for a relocation company. My responsibilities entailed helping newly arrived expatriates integrate into Hong Kong, and I enjoyed the freedom it offered, as it wasn't full-time.

I just didn't feel ready to have kids, but in my culture, the moment you got married, you were expected to produce children. I often found myself torn between external expectations and what I really wanted to do, and I sometimes felt almost inadequate among my friends for not wanting the same things they did, especially because of my desire to delay having children.

Members of our community kept reminding me that as women, we had a body clock running against us, which did nothing but feed the fear already living inside me—old worries, starting with my anxiety over being too much trouble because I was a girl, being wrong because I didn't fit in anywhere. I recall thinking, *But if we really want children, we can always adopt! There are so many unwanted children in the world who'd love to be given a home. Plus, I wouldn't have to worry about a biological clock!*

Danny and I actually discussed this seriously, and we both agreed that adoption made a lot of sense. It would also remove the pressure of having to be a slave to my own body. However, whenever I mentioned the possibility to others in our community, I always received negative responses. The most common was: "Can't you bear children? Oh, I'm so sorry."

Once again, I found the old fear of not "measuring up" rearing its head within me . . . but my focus on that subject came to an end all too quickly.

During the summer of 2001, my best friend, Soni, was diagnosed with cancer, and the news shocked me to the core. She had difficulty breathing one day, and when she went for a checkup, they found that she had a large tumor in her thorax, pushing against her lungs. I just couldn't believe this could happen to her. She was young, strong, vibrant, healthy, and had so much to live for. The doctors had her admitted to the hospital right away for surgery to remove the mass, followed by radiation treatment and chemotherapy.

Then, within a few months of Soni's diagnosis, we received news that Danny's brother-in-law (his younger sister's husband) had been diagnosed with an aggressive form of cancer.

This news instilled a deep fear in me because both of them were close to my age. I began researching everything I could about cancer and its causes. Initially, I started doing this in the hope of helping, because I wanted to be there for Soni, to help her fight. But I found that the more I read about the disease, the more I was afraid of everything that could potentially cause it. I started to believe that everything created cancer—pesticides, microwaves, preservatives, genetically modified foods, sunshine, air pollution, plastic food containers, mobile phones, and so on. This progressed until eventually, I started to fear life itself.

APRIL 26, 2002 IS A DAY NEITHER DANNY nor I will forget easily. Hesitantly, we walked into the doctor's office as though entering a house of death. Fear crept in around us, warning that a shock waited around every corner. It was late Friday afternoon, the last day of work before sharing a weekend together. We wove our way through the rush, as everyone was starting to leave work to celebrate the pre-weekend happy hour—everyone, that is, but us. We scarcely noticed the setting orange sun casting its fiery glow on the glass skyscrapers of our vibrant city as it lowered itself behind the harbor. Today we were to learn the results of the tests the doctor had run on me.

A few days earlier, I'd found a lump on my right shoulder just above the collarbone. In that moment, I refused—rather, I *demanded* that it be nothing more than a cyst or large boil. Yet the ugly little voice in the back of my mind, a predictor of doom, harped at me relentlessly, convincing me it was more than that.

Over the previous few months, I'd been tearfully visiting my friend Soni as she lay dying in the hospital from cancer diagnosed the year before. In terror and sorrow, I watched her body, being eaten alive inch by inch, consumed by a beast that refused to be tamed, even by the most advanced medical science available. I couldn't allow myself to think of that horror happening to me. Still, the lump at the base of my neck forced me to face the possibility and have it checked out. I'd had a biopsy, and I was getting the results that day.

The doctor was very gentle and kind as he broke the news: "You have lymphoma, which is a form of cancer of the lymphatic system." But from the instant he uttered the word *cancer*, I didn't hear much more of what he was saying. His voice came to me as though he were under water. My eyes glazed over and rested on the view from the clinic window. Outside, nothing had changed: The sun continued its journey, slowly setting behind the harbor; the skyscrapers glowed in muted hues of orange and amber; and people went on their way to the laughter and joy of happy hour. Yet learning the reality of what was happening within me had instantaneously changed my whole world.

Sympathetically, the doctor went through the options available. "I will stick by you," he assured me, "no matter what decision you make, what treatment option you choose. But first, I'm booking you for a scan for Monday morning so that we can 'stage' your diagnosis—find out what stage the cancer is. After the scan, come and see me, and we'll discuss your results."

His voice was a muffled roar in my head, and I shoved away his advice. I could barely hear him tell us to try to relax and enjoy the weekend as best as we could.

Terror collided violently with reason. Neither Danny nor I could think. We refused to. We didn't want to think about cancer, about options, about death! I wanted to pull the normal world around me and run away. Indeed, I could not consider—was not capable of considering—the options. That was too scary, and my brain swirled in confusion. Luckily, the doctor had said that we didn't need to make any decisions until Monday morning, when I was scheduled to have the MRI scan and talk to him about my ongoing treatment.

Although my mind was far away and I had so many questions, Danny had convinced me to go out on a date and leave the world behind. So when we returned home, I got into my favorite coral-red dress. As I stood there all dressed up, my husband put his arms around me and said, "Don't be scared. We'll get through this together."

So that evening, we ran away . . . at least for a while.

We dined under the stars at El Cid, my favorite outdoor restaurant, right by the Stanley Bay waterfront on the south side of Hong Kong Island. The moon shone in its glorious fullness, while a gentle sea breeze fluttered through the air. The soft sounds of waves from the nearby ocean complemented the music from the mariachi band that serenaded from table to table. To ensure a perfect night, we tipped the band so that they'd stay by us for the longest time, performing my favorite songs. The sangria flowed, the musicians played, and we forgot about the world beyond our table.

The next morning, I awoke curled in Danny's arms. It was glorious to snuggle next to him and push away the world. I wanted the trip to the doctor's office to have simply been a bad dream, but reality shoved its repulsive head into my thoughts. I still had cancer and couldn't run from the knowledge. How was I to get away from my own body?

The games we have the ability to play in our minds amaze me. As Saturday morning meandered into afternoon, I didn't want anyone to know about the diagnosis. If no one found out, then I wouldn't have to deal with it. I could escape in my mind if not in my body.

"We're going to have to tell our families, you know," Danny said rationally.

"I know, but they'll all make such a big deal about the whole thing. Can I just have one more day of peace and solitude before we tell anyone?" I bargained.

That afternoon, however, my mother called to ask why she hadn't heard from me regarding the biopsy results. Danny broke the news to her, and the next thing I knew, she was booking a flight to come to Hong Kong. My brother called, telling me he was also making arrangements to come and be with me.

I didn't want them to take it so seriously; I didn't want all this drama. It made the situation so real! Their loving reactions shoved reality into my face like a cold, dead fish. There was no longer a way around the truth of the diagnosis.

ON MONDAY, DANNY AND I ONCE MORE found ourselves in the clinic, openly talking about the options. I'd just done the MRI, and the doctor was reviewing the results with a look of kind concern on his face.

"It's stage 2A," he said gently.

"What does that mean?" asked Danny.

"It means that it's spread down into the chest and under-arm area, but it's contained within the upper body," the doctor answered patiently. "Now, let's start looking at the options available to you. My suggestion would be possibly a combination of chemotherapy and radiation."

"I will not have chemotherapy!" I emphatically announced to the room.

"But darling, that's pretty well all that's open to us," Danny said in surprise, and I turned to him with a look of determination.

"Look what chemotherapy is doing to Soni, and how about your sister's husband?" I replied.

I didn't want to have this conversation. I wanted things to go back to the way they were. I buried my face in my hands and attempted to push away my thoughts.

"Do you really want me to die like that?" I could hear the terror in my voice. "They're just wasting away and . . . and in so much pain. I'd rather die this very moment than allow that to happen to me."

"I know," Danny said as he reached out and placed his gentle palm over my cold hand, which lay limply on the doctor's desk. "But I don't want to lose you. What else can be done?"

We'd been married six years. We had so many dreams to live for, places we wanted to go, and things we wanted to do. But like the crumbling glaciers of the north, our dreams seemed to dissolve before us.

In an attempt to pull myself away from my fears, I tried to reassure him: "There are other methods." I turned to the doctor, seeking support for my assertion. "I'm convinced there are ways to beat cancer without chemotherapy."

THAT DAY, DANNY AND I BEGAN A LONG JOURNEY. TOGETHER, we seemed to join the heroes of ancient mythology as we trekked onward, determined to beat this disease that was now starting to take over our lives. From the beginning, my journey was fraught with a roller coaster of emotions, ranging from hopefulness to disappointment, terror, and finally anger.

Prior to my diagnosis, one of my biggest fears in life had been getting cancer—it seemed to be occurring with more frequency to people I knew. Receiving my diagnosis as I was witnessing the disease claiming the lives of both my best friend and Danny's brother-in-law was just confirming my observation. I'd been watching helplessly as chemotherapy appeared to be destroying the very bodies that it was supposed to heal. And now, here it was invading our own lives . . . pillaging our world and ravaging all it found.

Thoughts of these ill loved ones sent rage and panic storming through me. The fear of cancer now gripped me in its vice; it seemed to shove my stomach into my throat with a clenched fist. The effects of chemotherapy frightened me even more. Every muscle tightened in a protective clamp and held onto life.

Over the months prior to my own diagnosis, I'd been watching Soni's health deteriorate rapidly. During that time, I'd constantly felt bad if I went out or had fun while she was sick in the hospital. It somehow felt wrong to be enjoying myself while she was suffering. As her health continued to deteriorate, it became more and more difficult for me to find enjoyment in life or free myself from the feelings of guilt.

Now that I was dealing with my own cancer, it became more and more difficult to watch my friend get sicker and sicker, and I found myself spending less time with her. When I saw Soni, I was unable to stay positive or optimistic for her, or even for myself. I reached a point where I didn't think it was helping either of us to spend as much time together as we used to. It frightened me just to observe what the cancer was doing to her body—as well as the effects of the treatment. I felt vulnerable at the thought that the same fate was possibly in store for me, and it was all just too much handle.

THE DAY I GOT A CALL FROM SONI'S SISTER TELLING ME that my best friend's battle was over, I broke down and wept. She'd finally left us.

Although I was overcome with emotion and ached at the thought that she was gone, a small part of me was relieved that she was no longer in pain.

The day of Soni's funeral will be etched in my memory forever. I still can see the look of devastation on the faces of her parents at losing their beloved daughter; the shock of her younger sister and older brother at losing their dear sibling; the grief and helplessness on her husband's face as he was coming to terms with his loss. But most of all, I'll never forget the tearstained, innocent faces of her little children and their look of horror as they watched their mother's coffin being thrown into the fires of the crematorium. That memory will haunt me until the end of my days. And that was the day that *anger* was added into the mix of my spectrum of emotions toward my plight.

And to make matters worse, it wasn't long after the funeral that we received the call telling us that Danny's brother-in-law had lost his battle as well. He, too, left behind a young spouse (Danny's younger sister) and two small children.

I was angry at the cruel joke we call life. I couldn't understand what it was all for. It seemed as though we lived for a few years; we learned from our struggles; and finally, when we got the hang of things, we ended up thrown on a fire in a wooden box. Surely it wasn't supposed to happen so soon. It all seemed so meaningless, somehow—so pointless.

CHAPTER 6

Seeking Salvation

Anger.

Dread.

Frustration.

Fear.

Desperation.

That was the spectrum of emotions that I dealt with following Soni's death. From morning to night, each day was an intense roller-coaster ride as I questioned, challenged, raged, and despaired over my situation. I felt these emotions not only for myself, but also for my family. I dreaded the thought of them having to deal with my death.

My fear and desperation continued to drive me to research everything I could about holistic health and well-being, including Eastern healing systems. I was seeing several specialists in natural disciplines, and I also participated in different types of healing modalities. I tried hypnotherapy, meditated, prayed, chanted mantras, and took Chinese herbal remedies. Finally, I quit my freelance work and traveled to India to follow the healing system of ayurveda, while Danny stayed in Hong Kong. He couldn't come with me because of his job, but he visited me twice, for two weeks each time. We also spoke on the phone almost every day because he wanted to be kept informed of how I was doing.

I went to the town of Pune, where my father had passed away, to learn more about yoga and ayurveda from one of the masters. I spent a total of six months in India, and during that time, I finally felt as though I were regaining my health. My yoga master put me through a grueling regimen. I had to follow a very specific diet of vegetarian food and herbal remedies, along with a routine of yoga *asanas* (poses) at sunrise and sunset.

I did this for months and actually started to feel much better. He was an amazing guru, who didn't even believe that I had cancer. I told him that the medical doctors had conducted tests and confirmed I had lymphoma, to which he said, "*Cancer* is just a word that creates fear. Forget about that word, and let's just focus on balancing your body. All illnesses are just symptoms of imbalance. No illness can remain when your entire system is in balance."

I really enjoyed my time under my yoga master's tutelage, and he helped alleviate my fears around cancer. At the end of six months, he was convinced that I was healed—and so was I. I felt victorious, as though I'd finally made the breakthrough, and I was anxious to go back home and reunite with Danny. I'd missed him terribly and had so much to share with him.

When I returned home to Hong Kong, at first many people remarked on how well I looked. I certainly felt better than I had in a long time, both physically and emotionally, but my jubilation was short-lived. It wasn't long before others wanted to know what I'd been doing for so long in India and how I'd healed. When I told them about my ayurvedic regimen, however, I received mainly fear-based and negative responses. These were well-meaning people who genuinely cared about me and my well-being, and they were skeptical about my choices, which is why they had such a great impact on me. Most believed that cancer couldn't be treated in that way, and I slowly felt the doubts and fear creeping back into my psyche as I defended my position.

In hindsight, when that began to happen, I should have gone back to India to regain my health again. Instead, I actually started to be influenced by the skepticism I was facing over my choice of treatment, so I remained in Hong Kong.

I attempted to understand Traditional Chinese Medicine (TCM), since it's commonly practiced here. However, because it conflicted so much with ayurveda, I was left feeling very confused. In ayurveda, you're encouraged to be vegetarian; whereas in TCM, you're encouraged to consume meat, particularly pork. In the Indian system, meats such as pork and beef are the worst things you can eat.

To make matters worse, I turned to Western naturopathy for help because I was so bewildered. This not only added to the confusion, but also increased my fears. I was getting conflicting messages from every discipline. In Western naturopathic systems, sugar and dairy are considered absolute no-nos—in fact, they're seen as foods that feed the growth of cancer cells. According to the systems I was researching, sugar feeds the mutated cells. In ayurveda, on the other hand, dairy is a must; and sugar and sweet foods are required as part of a balanced diet, based on balancing all the different taste buds.

So I became very stressed about food and was afraid of eating almost anything. I didn't know what was good for me and what wasn't, because each system of healing espoused a different truth, and they all conflicted with each other. This confusion only added to my already overwhelming fears. And as the terror tightly gripped me in its vice once more, I watched helplessly as my health rapidly deteriorated.

I FELT THE NEED TO BE ALONE MOST OF THE TIME and only let those closest to me into my life. I wanted to shut out reality in an attempt to shut out the truth. I couldn't bear how people looked at me and treated me. As my health declined, I didn't like the way others felt sorry for me and made allowances for me, as though I were different or not normal. I also felt very uncomfortable about the way those from my culture thought it was my karma—that I must have done something in a previous life to warrant this punishment. Because I, too, believed in karma, it made me feel as though

I had done something to be ashamed of in order to deserve this. It seemed as if I were being judged, and it also made me feel helpless.

If this is retribution for something I did in a previous life, I wondered, *how can I change it? What can I possibly do about it now?* Thoughts like this would leave me feeling completely hopeless about my situation.

But through all this, I put up a front. I laughed and smiled and made small talk, even when I didn't want to, because it was important to me not to cause concern or worry anyone else with my condition. I didn't want others to feel upset or uncomfortable because of my situation, so I continued to put the feelings and needs of everyone else before my own. So many people remarked on how "brave" I was, and how they admired the way I was dealing with my illness. Many, many individuals also commented on how positive and happy I always was—but that's not how I felt inside.

Danny was the only person who really understood what was going on and how much being around other people took a toll on me, so he slowly began acting as a protective shell around me, shutting people out. In the presence of others, I always felt the need to perform at being happy and positive, because I never wanted anyone to feel bad for me, nor did I want them to worry. Eventually, this started to really drain me, and I wouldn't even answer the phone because I didn't want to talk about my illness, I didn't want anybody's advice on how to handle what was going on inside me, and I didn't want to repeatedly answer the endless questions that people who care tend to ask.

I stopped going out and stayed in the safety of my own home, because apart from feeling unwell, I physically appeared very sick. My breathing was labored; my limbs were very, very thin; and I had difficulty holding my head up. The looks and comments I got because of this bothered me. I knew that people weren't staring at me out of contempt or displeasure, but rather out of curiosity and, perhaps, a sense of pity. When I caught them looking, they shifted their eyes away abruptly, and I sensed their discomfort. I recognized the emotion behind their expressions, as I'd often felt it myself when seeing someone who was ill. They felt sorry for me. I soon came to accept that reaction as the norm from people who saw or interacted with me, and *I* felt sorry that my presence made others feel so uncomfortable, so at this point I stopped going out in public altogether.

Soon, I found myself locked in my own cage of fear and desperation, where my experience of life was getting smaller and smaller. Time slid by in a slippery descent. To me, anyone who didn't have cancer was lucky. I envied every healthy person I met. It didn't matter what their living conditions were; they were without the fiend that was relentlessly plundering my body . . . my mind . . . my life.

Each morning, I woke up with a glimmer of hope: *Today may just be the day that things turn around.* But each evening would end with the familiar, heavy feeling, every night bringing a greater sense of defeat than the day before.

Disillusioned, I started to question what I was fighting so hard to keep. What did it all mean anyway? In my pain and fear, I could no longer see the purpose in continuing, and I felt myself getting tired. I was beginning to give up. I was getting ready to admit that I was beaten.

BY THIS TIME, I WAS GOING IN AND OUT OF THE HOSPITAL for blood transfusions and other treatments. When I was at home, I spent most of my days sleeping or resting. I couldn't go out or walk around for prolonged periods of time. Just half an hour of activity left me tired and out of breath. I was losing weight fast and perpetually running a low-grade fever.

"Do you think my condition can still improve at this stage?" I asked my doctor one day, immediately after he'd finished conducting a routine body scan to assess my situation.

He averted his eyes as he said, "I'll send the nurse in to help you get dressed." What he didn't tell me was that he wanted to talk to Danny in private.

"There's little we can do now," the doctor told him once they were safely outside. He looked directly at my husband and continued, "She has about three months to live at best. The latest scans show that the tumors have grown and increased in number, and the cancer has spread quite aggressively throughout her lymphatic system. It's too late even for chemotherapy—her body can't handle the toxicity at this stage. She's so weak that any treatment now will just weaken her further and bring her closer to death. I'm so sorry."

Although Danny put on a brave front and didn't tell me what the doctor had said at that time (he shared it with me many months later), I could tell something wasn't right. At that point, he'd barely been going to work, but from the day of that doctor's visit, he stopped going in altogether. He seemed reluctant to ever leave my side.

One day, I asked him, "Am I going to die?"

"We're all going to die sometime," he said.

"I know that, silly," I countered. "I mean now, because of the cancer. What if I die?"

"Then I'm going to come and get you, and bring you back," he responded gently, stroking my head as I lay on the bed.

This was about six weeks after the last meeting with the doctor. By now, breathing had become a labored task, and an oxygen tank was my permanent companion. I couldn't lie down, needing to be propped up at all times to keep from drowning in my own fluids. Every time I tried to lie flat, I started choking and had difficulty breathing, so changing my position in bed became an impossible task. My body broke out in lesions all over. So many toxins had invaded my system that my skin was forced to open and release the poisons within.

Many times I woke up in a heavy sweat, my clothes soaked through—night sweats being a common symptom of lymphoma. Often, my skin itched all over, as though ants were crawling all over me. I recall one night when the itching was so strong that no matter how much I scratched myself, it wouldn't subside. Danny got ice cubes from the freezer and put them into ziplock bags, and we rubbed these ice packs all over my legs, arms, and body in order to soothe my inflamed skin. It took a long time, but the itchiness finally subsided.

Most of our nights were sleepless, and by this point I was completely dependent on Danny to care for me. He anticipated my every need before it arose. He dressed my wounds and helped me wash my hair. Although I felt guilty about him having to spend his days caring for me in this way, I knew that he never, ever acted out of obligation, duty, or responsibility. Everything he did sprang from pure love for me.

My digestive system eventually stopped absorbing nutrients from the food I was eating, so I became malnourished. Danny bought my favorite chocolates, and my mother prepared some of my favorite foods to try to get me to eat, but I had no appetite. I wasn't absorbing whatever I did manage to choke down, and I watched my muscles disintegrate until I could no longer walk. My mobility then came in the form of a wheelchair. My body started to consume the protein from my own flesh to survive, until I looked like a poster child from a famine-struck nation. I became a skeleton of my old self, and my head felt like a 300-pound barbell that I could barely lift from the pillow.

I was still going in and out of the hospital, but every time I was there, I always wanted to leave as quickly as possible and be home. I felt those institutions were cold, clinical, and depressing, and they seemed to make me feel even sicker than I already was. So we hired a nurse to stay with me during the day.

Both my mother and my husband never left my side during those days, and Danny sat up with me through the night. He wanted to make sure that I continued to breathe, and to be there just in case I was taking my last breath. Many nights I wasn't able to sleep for coughing, so I was always grateful for his comforting presence. But I was also acutely aware of his pain, and that made it so much harder for me to endure my situation. Even through all of this, I continued to put on a brave front, and kept assuring everyone that I wasn't in pain. I told them that I was feeling fine even though that was so far from the truth!

At the same time, I was also aware of my mother's anguish. I knew that no mother should watch her child go before her, let alone witness her child's slow and painful disintegration.

ON THE MORNING OF FEBRUARY 1, 2006, I was feeling more positive than usual. I actually started to notice things around me. The sky looked bluer than normal, and the world seemed like a beautiful place. Although still wheelchair-bound, my oxygen tank as my constant companion, I was wheeled home from the clinic with a feeling that it was okay to let go now, that everything was going to be fine.

The world won't stop if I'm not in it. I have nothing to worry about. I don't understand why, but I'm feeling emotionally good. Better than I've felt in a long time, I recall thinking.

My body ached, and my breathing was difficult and labored, so I went to bed. Because I was in pain all over and couldn't sleep, the nurse administered morphine just before she left at the end of the day so that I could get some rest. But something was different. I could feel myself relaxing and letting go of the strong grip with which I'd been clinging to life. All that time, it was as though I'd been hanging from the edge of a cliff. I'd been fighting a losing battle, struggling to hold on. I was finally ready to let go of everything that I'd been gripping so tightly. I felt myself sink into a deep sleep.

The following morning, February 2, I didn't open my eyes. Apparently, my face was grossly swollen. So were my arms, legs, hands, and feet. Danny took one look at me and called the doctor, who directed him to rush me to the hospital.

I was about to end my battle with cancer.

PART II

MY JOURNEY TO DEATH . . . AND BACK

CHAPTER 7

Leaving the World Behind

As I was being rushed to the hospital, the world around me started to appear surreal and dreamlike, and I could feel myself slip further and further away from consciousness. I arrived at the hospital in a coma, only to find that the doctors were bleak—if not hopeless—in their evaluation of my chances. This wasn't the same place where I'd usually visited for my treatments throughout the duration of my illness. The facility I'd been going to over the years was more like a large clinic than a full-blown hospital. It had been adequate for what my doctor prescribed in the past, but it wasn't equipped to deal with medical emergencies. It was my choice all along to be treated at the smaller neighborhood institution because it was less intimidating—and I absolutely hated hospitals. I feared them because of the two people I'd lost. My best friend and Danny's brother-in-law both died in large, cancer-specialist hospitals.

But when Danny called the clinic the morning I fell into a coma, my doctor told him to rush me to one of the largest and best-equipped hospitals in Hong Kong, where the doctor would have a team of specialists waiting for me. So this was the first time I was in this particular place and the first time I was being treated by this particular medical team

The moment the oncologist saw me, her face visibly filled with shock.

"Your wife's heart may still be beating," she told Danny, "but she's not really in there. It's too late to save her."

Who's the doctor talking about? I wondered. *I've never felt better in my life! And why do Mum and Danny look so frightened and worried? Mum, please don't cry. What's wrong? Are you crying because of me? Don't cry! I'm fine—really, dear Mama, I am!* I thought I was speaking these words aloud, but nothing came out. I had no voice.

I wanted to hug my mother, comfort her and tell her that I was fine; and I couldn't comprehend why I was unable to do so. Why was my physical body not cooperating? Why was I just lying there, limp, when all I wanted to do was to hug my beloved husband and mother, assuring them that I was fine and no longer in pain?

Because of the gravity of the situation, the doctor immediately called for another senior oncologist to back her up. In this near-death state, I was more acutely aware of all that was going on around me than I've ever been in a normal physical state. I wasn't using my five biological senses, yet I was keenly taking everything in, much more so than if I'd been using my physical organs. It was as though another, completely different type of perception kicked in, and more than just *perceive*, I seemed to also encompass everything that was happening, as though I was slowly *merging* with it all.

The senior oncologist immediately ordered a medical team to wheel my gurney to the radiology lab so that they could do a full-body scan. I noticed that my head was still propped up at an angle with pillows, just as it had been at home the last few days. This was because, as I described earlier, my lungs were so filled with fluid that if my head lay flat, I'd choke on my own fluids.

I was still connected to the portable oxygen tank, and when I reached the radiology lab, they removed the mask from my face, lifted me up, and put me in the MRI machine. Within a few seconds, I started choking, coughing, and sputtering.

"Please don't remove the oxygen—and she can't lie down flat! Please, she's choking! She can't breathe! She's going to die if you do this!" I heard Danny cry out to the medical team.

"We really need to do this," explained one of the radiologists. "Please don't worry. We'll be as gentle as we can. She can handle about 30 seconds off the oxygen at a time."

So the radiologist slid me out of the MRI capsule every 30 or 40 seconds to put the oxygen mask over my face, then removed it and slid me back in again. As a result, the scan took a very long time to complete. After they finished, they wheeled me to the intensive care unit (ICU).

The medical team took what action they could, spurred on by my husband's insistence that they not give up on me. While the minutes ticked by, I lay in the ICU as the staff administered treatments by way of needles and tubes, and my helpless family looked on.

A thick curtain was then drawn all around my bed, separating me from the patients on either side of me. Danny and my mother were both on the outside of the cubicle created by the curtain.

I noticed that the nurses were still scurrying around, preparing to hook up my near-lifeless body to the hospital's oxygen and other machinery to start an intravenous flow of fluids and glucose, since I was seriously malnourished. There was a monitor above my bed, and they started connecting me so that they could measure my blood pressure and heart rate. A food tube was inserted through my nose, down the back of my throat, and into my stomach so that I could be fed directly, and oxygen was being pumped through my nose via a respirator. They had trouble inserting the food tube and sliding it down my trachea, so they sprayed something down my throat to numb the muscles, and were then able to push the tube down more easily.

I knew when people came in to see me, who they were and what they were doing. Although my physical eyes were closed, I seemed to be acutely aware of every minute detail that was taking place around me and beyond. The sharpness of my perception was even more intense than if I'd been awake and using my physical senses. I seemed to just know and understand everything—not only what was going on around me, but also what everyone was feeling, as though I were able to see and feel through each person.

I was able to sense their fears, their hopelessness, and their resignation to my situation.

Danny and Mum look so sad and frightened. I wish they could know that I'm no longer in pain—I wish I could tell them. Mum, please don't cry! I'm fine! I'm right here. I'm with you now!

I was fully aware of what was going on around me. Although everything seemed to be happening at the same time, whatever I focused on would become clear in that moment.

"I can't find her veins!" I heard one of the nurses saying frantically to the doctor on duty. There was fear in that voice. "They've completely retracted. Oh, just look at her limbs! There's no flesh on them. Her body hasn't been absorbing nutrition for a while." I clearly recall that this was a male voice—a male nurse.

He sounds so hopeless, I thought. *He's ready to give up on me, and I don't blame him.*

"Her lungs are filled with liquid. She's drowning in her own fluid. I'll have to tap it out of her lungs so that she can at least start to breath with more ease." That was the senior oncologist speaking. I watched as they worked with great purpose over my motionless body—a form that seemed too small to contain how I was feeling about myself in that moment.

Although the medical team moved with great speed, and there was a sense of urgency in their actions, I also sensed an air of acceptance, as though they'd come to terms with the fact that it was too late to change my fate. I was extremely aware of every detail, but I couldn't physically feel anything—anything, that is, except a release and a level of freedom I'd never known before.

Wow, this is incredible! I feel so free and light! What's going on? I've never felt this good! There are no more tubes, no more wheelchair. I can move around freely now without any help! And my breathing is no longer labored—how amazing this is!

I felt no emotional attachment to my seemingly lifeless body as it lay there on the hospital bed. It didn't feel as though it were mine. It looked far too small and insignificant to have housed what I was experiencing. I felt free, liberated, and magnificent.

Every pain, ache, sadness, and sorrow was gone! I felt completely unencumbered. I couldn't recall feeling this way before—not ever.

It was as though I'd been a prisoner in my own body for the past four years as the cancer ravaged my physical form, and at last I was being released. I was tasting freedom for the first time! I began to feel weightless and to become aware that I was able to be anywhere at any time . . . and this didn't seem unusual. It felt normal, as though this were the real way to perceive things. I didn't even think it odd that I was aware of my husband and the doctor speaking to each other outside the ICU, some 40 feet down a hallway.

"There's nothing we can do for your wife, Mr. Moorjani. Her organs have already shut down. She has tumors the size of lemons throughout her lymphatic system, from the base of her skull to below her abdomen. Her brain is filled with fluid, as are her lungs. Her skin has developed lesions that are weeping with toxins. She won't even make it through the night," the man told Danny. This doctor was someone I'd never seen before.

I watched as Danny's face change to anguish, and wanted to cry out to him, *It's okay, darling—I'm okay! Please don't worry. Don't listen to the doctor. What they said isn't true!* But I couldn't. Nothing came out. He couldn't hear me.

"I don't want to lose her. I'm not ready to lose her," Danny said.

Although I wasn't filled with any attachment to my body, I felt a deep pull on my emotions to the drama that was unfolding around my inert form. More than anything, I wanted to relieve Danny of the deep despair he was experiencing at the thought of losing me.

Darling, can you hear me? Please listen! I want you to know that I'm okay!

As soon as I began to get emotionally attached to the drama taking place around me, I also felt myself being simultaneously pulled away, as though there were a bigger picture, a grander plan that was unfolding. I could feel my attachment recede as I began to know that everything was perfect and going according to plan.

As my emotions were being drawn away from my surroundings, I started to notice how I was continuing to expand to fill every space, until there was no separation between me and everything else. I encompassed—no, *became*—everything and everyone. I was fully aware of every word of the conversation that was taking place between my family and the doctors, although it was physically some distance away, outside my room. I knew the frightened expression on my husband's face and could feel his fear. It was as though, in that instant, I became him.

Simultaneously, although I hadn't known of it previously, I became aware that my brother, Anoop, was thousands of miles away on an airplane, anxiously coming to see me. Upon seeing him and his worried look, I once again felt myself being drawn back into the emotional drama of the physical realm.

Oh wow, there's Anoop! He's on an airplane. Why does he seem so anxious? It looks as though he's coming to Hong Kong to see me!

I recall *feeling* his sense of urgency to reach me. I felt an intense rush of emotion toward him.

Oh, poor Anoop. He's worried about me, and he wants to get here before I die. Don't worry, Anoop. I'll be here for you. You don't have to hurry! I'm not in pain anymore, dear brother!

I wanted to reach out and give him a hug and assure him that I was okay, and I couldn't understand why I wasn't able to reach out to him.

I'm here, bro!

I recall knowing that I didn't want my physical body to be dead before he arrived. I was aware of how that would make him feel, and I didn't want him to go through that.

But yet again, as my affection for my brother started to take over and I was becoming overwhelmed with not wanting him to experience the pain of his little sister dying, I found myself being simultaneously drawn away. Each time my emotions took over the situation, I discovered myself starting to expand again, and I felt a release from all attachment. Once more, I was surrounded by the reassuring feeling of a greater tapestry unfolding, where everything was exactly as it should be in the grand scheme of things.

THE FURTHER OUTWARD I EXPANDED, THE LESS UNUSUAL it felt to be in this miraculous state—in fact, I had no awareness of it being out of the ordinary. It all seemed perfectly natural to me at the time. I continued to be fully aware of every detail of every procedure that was being administered to me, while to the outside world I appeared to be in a coma.

I continued to sense myself expanding further and further outward, drawing away from my physical surroundings. It was as though I were no longer restricted by the confines of space and time, and continued to spread myself out to occupy a greater expanse of consciousness. I felt a sense of freedom and liberation that I'd never experienced in my physical life before. I can only describe this as the combination of a sense of joy mixed with a generous sprinkling of jubilation and happiness. It stemmed from being released from my sick and dying body, a feeling of jubilant emancipation from all the pain that my illness had caused me.

As I continued to plunge deeper into the other realm, expanding outward, becoming everyone and everything, I felt all my emotional attachments to my loved ones and my surroundings slowly fall away. What I can only describe as superb and glorious unconditional love surrounded me, wrapping me tight as I continued to let go. The term *unconditional love* really doesn't do justice to the feeling, as these words have been overused to the point of having lost their intensity. But the physical battle I'd fought for so very long had finally released its strong hold on me, and I had a beautiful experience of freedom.

It didn't feel as though I'd *physically* gone somewhere else—it was more as though I'd *awakened*. Perhaps I'd finally been roused from a bad dream. My soul was finally realizing its true magnificence! And in doing so, it was expanding beyond my body and this physical world. It extended further and further outward until it encompassed not only this existence, but continued to expand into another realm that was beyond this time and space, and at the same time included it.

Love, joy, ecstasy, and awe poured into me, through me, and engulfed me. I was swallowed up and enveloped in more love than

I ever knew existed. I felt more free and alive than I ever had. As I described, I suddenly *knew* things that weren't physically possible, such as the conversations between medical staff and my family that were taking place far away from my hospital bed.

The overwhelming sensations were in a realm of their own, and words don't exist to describe them. The feeling of complete, pure, unconditional *love* was unlike anything I'd known before. Unqualified and nonjudgmental . . . it was totally undiscriminating, as if I didn't have to do anything to deserve it, nor did I need to prove myself to earn it.

To my amazement, I became aware of the presence of my father, who'd died ten years earlier, and it brought me an unbelievable level of comfort to sense him with me.

Dad, you're here! I can't believe it!

I wasn't speaking those words, I was merely *thinking* them—in fact, it was more like I was feeling the emotions behind the words, as there was no other way of communicating in that realm other than through our emotions.

Yes, I'm here, my darling, and I've always been here—for you and our whole family! my father communicated to me. Again, there were no words, just emotions, but I clearly understood.

And then I recognized the essence of my best friend, Soni, who'd died of cancer three years prior. I felt what I can only describe as excitement as their presence enveloped me like a warm embrace, and I was comforted. I seemed to *know* that they'd been around me for some time, long before I became aware of them, all through my illness.

I was also aware of other beings around me. I didn't recognize them, but I knew they loved me very much and were protecting me. I realized that they were there all the time, surrounding me with so much love, even when I wasn't conscious of it.

It was tremendously comforting for me to reconnect with Soni's essence, for I'd missed her so much during the years since she'd gone. I felt nothing but unconditional love, both from her and for her. And then, just as I experienced that, it was as though my essence merged with Soni's and I *became* her. I understood that she was here, there, and everywhere. She was able to be in all places at all times for all her loved ones.

Although I was no longer using my five physical senses, I had unlimited perception, as if a new sense had become available, one that was more heightened than any of our usual faculties. I had 360-degree peripheral vision with total awareness of my surroundings. And as amazing as it all sounds, it still felt almost normal. Being in a body now felt confining.

Time felt different in that realm, too, and I felt all moments at once. I was aware of *everything* that pertained to me—past, present, and future—simultaneously. I became conscious of what seemed to be simultaneous lives playing out. I seemed to have a younger brother in one incarnation, and I was protective of him. But I knew that this sibling's essence was the same as Anoop's, only in that existence, he was younger instead of older than I was. This life I was now perceiving with Anoop seemed to take place in an underdeveloped rural setting, in a time and location I couldn't identify. We were living in a sparsely furnished mud hut, and I looked after Anoop while our parents went out to work in the fields.

As I was experiencing the sensations associated with being a protective older sister, ensuring that there was enough for us to eat and we were safe from any undesirable external elements, it didn't feel like a *past* life. Even though the scene appeared historical, in that realm, it still felt as though it were happening here and now.

In other words, time didn't run linearly the way we experience it here. It's as though our earthly minds convert what happens around us into a sequence; but in actuality, when we're not expressing through our bodies, everything occurs simultaneously, whether past, present, or future.

Although being able to perceive all points of time simultaneously lent to the atmosphere of clarity in that realm, recalling it and writing about it creates confusion. The sequence isn't obvious when there's no linear time, making the retelling sound clumsy.

It seems as though our five senses limit us to focus only on one point in time at any given moment, and we string these together to create an illusion of linear reality. Our physicality also limits our perception of the space around us, confining us to only what our eyes and ears can see and hear or to what we can touch, smell, or taste. However, without the limitations of my body, I took in all points of time and space as they pertained to me, all at once.

MY HEIGHTENED AWARENESS IN THAT EXPANDED realm was indescribable, despite my best efforts to explain it. The clarity was amazing.

The universe makes sense! I realized. *I finally understand—I know why I have cancer!* I was too caught up in the wonder of that moment to dwell on the cause, although I'd soon examine it more closely. I also seemed to comprehend why I'd come into this life in the first place—I knew my true purpose.

Why do I suddenly understand all this? I wanted to know. *Who's giving me this information? Is it God? Krishna? Buddha? Jesus?* And then I was overwhelmed by the realization that God isn't a *being*, but a *state of being . . . and I was now that state of being!*

I saw my life intricately woven into everything I'd known so far. My experience was like a single thread woven through the huge and complexly colorful images of an infinite tapestry. All the other threads and colors represented my relationships, including every life I'd touched. There were threads representing my mother, my father, my brother, my husband, and every other person who'd ever come into my life, whether they related to me in a positive or negative way.

Oh my, there's even a thread for Billy, who bullied me as a child!

Every single encounter was woven together to create the fabric that was the sum of my life up to this point. I may have been only one thread, yet I was integral to the overall finished picture.

Seeing this, I understood that I owed it to myself, to everyone I met, and to life itself to always be an expression of my own unique essence. Trying to be anything or anyone else didn't make me better—it just deprived me of my true self! It kept others from experiencing me for who I am, and it deprived me of interacting authentically with them. Being inauthentic also deprives the universe of who I came here to be and what I came here to express.

In that state of clarity, I also realized that I'm not who I'd always thought I was: *Here I am without my body, race, culture, religion, or beliefs . . . yet I continue to exist! Then what am I? Who am I? I certainly don't feel reduced or smaller in any way. On the contrary, I haven't ever been this huge, this powerful, or this all-encompassing. Wow, I've never, ever felt this way!*

There I was, without my body or any of my physical traits, yet my pure essence continued to exist, and it was *not* a reduced element of my whole self. In fact, it felt far greater and more intense and expansive than my physical being—magnificent, in fact. I felt eternal, as if I'd always existed and always would without beginning or end. I was filled with the knowledge that I was simply magnificent!

How have I never noticed this about myself before? I wondered.

As I looked at the great tapestry that was the accumulation of my life up to that point, I was able to identify exactly what had brought me to where I was today.

Just look at my life path! Why, oh why, have I always been so harsh with myself? Why was I always beating myself up? Why was I always forsaking myself? Why did I never stand up for myself and show the world the beauty of my own soul?

Why was I always suppressing my own intelligence and creativity to please others? I betrayed myself every time I said yes when I meant no! Why have I violated myself by always needing to seek approval from others just to be myself? Why haven't I followed my own beautiful heart and spoken my own truth?

Why don't we realize this when we're in our physical bodies? How come I never knew that we're not supposed to be so tough on ourselves?

I still felt myself completely enveloped in a sea of unconditional love and acceptance. I was able to look at myself with fresh eyes, and I saw that I was a beautiful being of the Universe. I understood that just the fact that I existed made me worthy of this tender regard rather than judgment. I didn't need to do anything specific; I deserved to be loved simply because I existed, nothing more and nothing less.

This was a rather surprising realization for me, because I'd always thought I needed to work at being lovable. I believed that I somehow had to be deserving and worthy of being cared for, so it was incredible to realize this wasn't the case. I'm loved unconditionally, for no other reason than simply because I exist.

I was transformed in unimaginable clarity as I realized that this expanded, magnificent essence was really me. It was the truth of my being. The understanding was so clear: I was looking into a new paradigm of self, becoming the crystalline light of my own awareness. Nothing interfered with the flow, glory, and amazing beauty of what was taking place.

I BECAME AWARE THAT WE'RE ALL connected. This was not only every person and living creature, but the interwoven unification felt as though it were expanding outward to include *everything* in the universe—every human, animal, plant, insect, mountain, sea, inanimate object, and the cosmos. I realized that the entire universe is alive and infused with consciousness, encompassing all of life and nature. Everything belongs to an infinite Whole. I was intricately, inseparably enmeshed with all of life. We're all facets of that unity—we're *all* One, and each of us has an effect on the collective Whole.

I knew that Danny's life and purpose were inextricably linked to mine, and that if I died, he'd follow me soon after. But I understood that even if this were to happen, everything would still be perfect in the bigger picture.

I also understood that the cancer was not some punishment for anything I'd done wrong, nor was I experiencing negative karma as a result of any of my actions, as I'd previously believed. It was as though every moment held infinite possibilities, and where I was at that point in time was a culmination of every decision, every choice, and every thought of my entire life. My many fears and my great power had manifested as this disease.

CHAPTER 8

Something Infinite
and Altogether Fantastic

Although I try to share my near-death experience here, there are no words that can come close to describing its depth and the amount of knowledge that came flooding through. So the best way to express it is through the use of metaphors and analogies. Hopefully, they capture a part of the essence of what I'm trying to convey at least in some small way.

Imagine, if you will, a huge, dark warehouse. You live there with only one flashlight to see by. Everything you know about what's contained within this enormous space is what you've seen by the beam of one small flashlight. Whenever you want to look for something, you may or may not find it, but that doesn't mean the thing doesn't exist. It's there, but you just haven't shone your light on it. And even when you do, the object you see may be difficult to make out. You may get a fairly clear idea of it, but often you're left wondering. You can only see what your light is focused on, and only identify that which you already know.

That is what physical life is like. We're only aware of what we focus our senses on at any given time, and we can only understand what is already familiar.

Next, imagine that one day, someone flicks on a switch. There for the first time, in a sudden burst of brilliance and sound and color, you can see the entire warehouse, and it's nothing like anything you'd ever imagined. Lights are blinking, flashing, glowing, and shooting sparks of red, yellow, blue, and green. You see colors you don't recognize, ones you've never seen before. Music floods the room with fantastic, kaleidoscopic, surround-sound melodies you've never heard before.

Neon signs pulse and boogie in rainbow strobes of cherry, lemon, vermillion, grape, lavender, and gold. Electric toys run on tracks up, down, and around shelves stacked with indescribable colored boxes, packages, papers, pencils, paints, inks, cans of food, packages of multihued candies, bottles of effervescent sodas, chocolates of every possible variety, champagne, and wines from every corner of the world. Skyrockets suddenly explode in starbursts, setting off sparkling flowers, cascades of cold fire, whistling embers, and animations of light.

The vastness, complexity, depth, and breadth of everything going on around you is almost overwhelming. You can't see all the way to the end of the space, and you know there's more to it than what you can take in from this torrent that's tantalizing your senses and emotions. But you do get a strong feeling that you're actually part of something alive, infinite, and altogether fantastic, that you are part of a large and unfolding tapestry that goes beyond sight and sound.

You understand that what you used to think was your reality was, in fact, hardly a speck within the vast wonder that surrounds you. You can see how all the various parts are interrelated, how they all play off each other, how everything fits. You notice just how many different things there are in the warehouse that you'd never seen, never even dreamed of existing in such splendor and glory of color, sound, and texture—but here they are, along with everything you already knew. And even the objects you were aware of have an entirely new context so that they, too, seem completely new and strangely superreal.

Even when the switch goes back off, nothing can take away your understanding and clarity, the wonder and beauty, or the fabulous aliveness of the experience. Nothing can ever cancel your knowledge of all that exists in the warehouse. You're now far more aware of what's there, how to access it, and what's possible than you ever were with your little flashlight. And you're left with a sense of awe over everything you experienced in those blindingly lucid moments. Life has taken on a different meaning, and your new experiences moving forward are created from this awareness.

I WONDERED AT MY NEWFOUND UNDERSTANDING in the other realm, enjoying and exploring that all-encompassing consciousness. As I did so, I became aware that I had a choice to make.

I reached a point where I once again strongly sensed the comforting presence of my father surrounding me, almost as if he were embracing me.

Dad, it feels like I've come home! I'm so glad to be here. Life is so painful! I told him.

But you're always home, darling, he impressed upon me. *You always were, and you always will be. I want you to remember that.*

Even though I hadn't always been close to my father while I was growing up, all I could feel emanating from him now was glorious, unconditional love. During my physical life with him, I'd often been frustrated by his attempts to make me conform to Indian cultural norms, such as trying to get me married young and making me feel like a misfit because I didn't always comply. But in this realm, I became aware that without any physical restrictions or the ties of all his cultural conditioning and expectations, all he had for me was pure love.

The cultural pressures he'd put on me during life had all dropped away, because they were all only part of physical existence. None of that mattered after death; those values didn't carry through into the afterlife. The only thing that remained was our connection and the unconditional love we had for each other. So for the first time, I actually felt cherished and safe in my father's presence. It truly felt amazing, as though I'd finally come home!

Our communication wasn't verbal, but a complete melding of mutual comprehension. It wasn't just that I *understood* my father— it was as though I *became* him. I was aware that he'd been with my entire family all through the years after he'd passed. He'd been with my mother, supporting her and watching over her; and he'd also been with me through my wedding and my illness.

I became aware that the essence of my father was communicating with me more directly: *Sweetheart, I want you to know that it's not your time to come home yet. But it's still your choice whether you want to come with me or go back into your body.*

But my body is so sick, drained, and ridden with cancer! was the immediate thought that came flooding through me. *Why would I want to go back to that body? It has caused nothing but suffering—not only for me, but for Mum and Danny, too! I can't see any purpose in going back.*

Not to mention that the state of unconditional love was just so blissful, I couldn't bear the thought of returning. I wanted to stay where I was forever and ever.

What subsequently happened is incredibly hard to describe. First, it felt as though whatever I directed my awareness toward appeared before me. Second, time was completely irrelevant. It wasn't even a factor to consider, as though it didn't exist.

Prior to this point, doctors had conducted tests on the functioning of my organs, and their report had already been written. But in that realm, it seemed as though the outcome of those tests and the report depended on the decision I had yet to make—whether to live or continue onward into death. If I chose death, the test results would indicate organ failure. If I chose to come back into physical life, they'd show my organs beginning to function again.

At that moment, I decided that I didn't want to return. I then became conscious of my physical body dying, and I saw the doctors speaking with my family, explaining that it was death due to organ failure.

At the same time, my father communicated with me, *This is as far as you can go, sweetheart. If you go any further, you cannot turn back.*

I became aware of a boundary before me, although the demarcation wasn't physical. It was more like an invisible threshold marked by a variation in energy levels. I knew that if I crossed it, there was no turning back. All my ties with the physical would be permanently severed; and as I'd seen, my family would be told that my death was the result of organ failure caused by end-stage lymphoma.

The unconditional love and acceptance was incredible, and I wanted to cross the threshold in order to continue to experience it for eternity. It was as though I was enveloped in the oneness, the pure essence of every living being and creature, without their aches, pains, dramas, and egos.

I turned my awareness toward my distraught family's reaction to the news of my death. I saw Danny's head buried in my lifeless chest, holding my frail hand. His body was shaking with deep and inconsolable sobs. My mother stood over me, looking white as a sheet in disbelief. And my brother, Anoop, arrived to the shock that he didn't make it in time.

Before I became sucked into what was going on with my physical existence and my family, however, I found myself being drawn away from my emotions. Once again, I was surrounded by the reassuring feeling of a greater story unfolding. I knew that even if I chose not to go back, everything was exactly as it should be in the grand tapestry of life.

In the moment that I made the decision to go on toward death, I became aware of a new level of truth.

I discovered that since I'd realized who I really was and understood the magnificence of my true self, if I chose to go back to life, my body would heal rapidly—not in months or weeks, but in days! I *knew* that the doctors wouldn't be able to find a trace of cancer if I chose to go back into my body!

How can that be? I was astounded by this revelation, and wanted to understand why.

It was then that I understood that my body is only a reflection of my internal state. If my inner self were aware of its greatness and connection with All-that-is, my body would soon reflect that and heal rapidly.

Even though I always had a choice, I also discerned that there was something more. . . . *It feels as though I have a purpose of some sort yet to fulfill. But what is it? How do I go about finding it?*

I perceived that I wouldn't have to go out and search for what I was supposed to do—it would unfold before me. It involved helping lots of people—thousands, maybe tens of thousands, perhaps to share a message with them. But I wouldn't have to pursue anything or work at figuring out how I was going to achieve that. I simply had to allow it to unfold.

To access this state of allowing, the only thing I had to do was *be myself!* I realized that all those years, all I *ever* had to do was be myself, without judgment or feeling that I was flawed. At the same time, I understood that at the core, our essence is made of pure love. *We are pure love*—every single one of us. How can we not be, if we come from the Whole and return to it? I knew that realizing this meant never being afraid of who we are. Therefore, being love and being our true self is one and the same thing!

As I experienced my biggest revelation, it felt like a bolt of lightning. I understood that merely by being the love I truly am, I would heal both myself and others. I'd never understood this before, yet it seemed so obvious. If we're all One, all facets of the same Whole, which is unconditional love, then of course *who we are is love!* I knew that was really the only purpose of life: to be our self, live our truth, and be the love that we are.

As though to confirm my realization, I became aware of both my father and Soni communicating to me: *Now that you know the truth of who you really are, go back and live your life <u>fearlessly</u>!*

CHAPTER 9

Realizing the Miracle

As I lay there in the hospital, even before anyone informed my brother that I was in a coma and my final stages of life, he sensed something was wrong. Anoop was living in Pune, India, and something compelled him to contact a travel agent and book a flight to Hong Kong. When he called, he requested a ticket for later that very day because he felt a sense of urgency. The agent said that flights out of Pune were already fully booked, but there was one from Mumbai. Anoop took it, and rented a car to drive the four hours to get on that flight to Hong Kong.

When Danny called my brother's home in Pune to inform him of my condition and tell him to come as soon as possible, my sister-in-law, Mona, picked up the phone and told Danny that Anoop was already on his way.

When Mona, who's Buddhist, became aware of just how dire my condition was, she urgently organized a group of fellow Buddhists to chant for my healing.

Meanwhile, here in Hong Kong, my mother was pacing up and down the corridor of the hospital, praying to Shiva for my life. She felt helpless, not knowing what more she could do, so she made her way to the Hindu temple—the very same one that my parents took me to as a child. She walked up the wide staircase at the entrance, through the courtyard, and into the main prayer hall where the large, life-size statues of the deities Krishna, Shiva, and Ganesha on their pedestals lined the front wall, painted and adorned in bright colors. My mother covered her head and sat before them with her head slightly bowed, speaking with them and drawing comfort from their presence.

At the same time, a close family friend of ours named Linda, who's a devout Catholic, organized a prayer group at her church. She told the priest about my situation, and they offered my name in prayer.

As I lay comatose on my bed, with all the tubes coming out of my nose, mouth, and arms, my husband stayed by my side, whispering to me in order to let me know that he was there, telling me to come back.

"We still have so much to do together, my darling," I could hear Danny whispering. "Please, *please* come back. I'm going to wait right here for you, even if it takes a lifetime."

He'd stayed awake the whole night, watching all the dials and meters above my bed, waiting, not wanting to miss it if I were to take my last breath, willing me to come back.

Dear, dear Danny. I hope you'll always know how much I love you, I found myself wanting to communicate with him. *Please don't worry about me. I'm fine. I wish I could share with you what I now know. That body whose hand you're holding isn't the real me. We'll always be together, connected through all of time and space. Nothing can separate us. Even if I physically die, we'll never be apart. Everything is perfect, just as it is. I know that now, and I want you to know it, too.*

Then, at about 4 a.m., my body suddenly started choking. I was gagging as though I couldn't get air. Danny panicked, thinking this was my last moment, and rang the emergency alarm. The nurses rushed in and agreed that I was choking, and one of them called the doctor. Then they turned my body around and started hitting me on my back.

It took about 20 minutes for the doctor to get there, and he told Danny that my lungs were filled with liquid, and I was choking on my own fluid. The doctor ordered the nurses to bring in a pleural-effusion kit. After they brought in what looked like a transparent bag with a long needle, he inserted the needle through my back and into my lung, drawing out some liquid, which drained into the transparent bag. He repeated this three or four times, until there was what looked like almost a liter of liquid in the bag, and then he removed the needle. I could still see my body, and it was breathing easier now.

My husband continued to stay at my bedside throughout the morning and well into the day, watching all the dials and meters above me and holding my hand.

My brother arrived in Hong Kong in the afternoon and called Danny from the airport on his mobile phone.

Danny told him, "Don't even go home to put your luggage down. Just come straight to the hospital in a taxi. We don't know how long we've got," so Anoop came straight to the hospital with his bags.

MY EYES STARTED TO FLICKER OPEN AROUND 4 P.M., and my vision was very blurred. I could barely see that the outline of the figure standing over me was Danny, and then I heard his voice: "She's back!"

He sounded so happy. It was the afternoon of February 3, about 30 hours after I'd entered the coma.

Then I heard my brother's voice, and I could feel myself trying to smile.

"Hey, sis! Welcome back!" Anoop said with audible joy.

"You made it!" I exclaimed. "I knew you were going to be here. I saw you coming on the plane."

He looked a little bewildered, but dismissed my comment. My family was just happy that I appeared to be coming around. My mother was there, too, smiling as she took my hand. I was confused because I didn't realize I'd been comatose, and I couldn't yet fully comprehend what was happening or understand that I was no longer in the other realm.

My vision was slowly becoming clearer, and I could make out my family more easily. I saw Anoop's suitcase just behind him against the wall.

The doctor walked in and looked both surprised and pleased to see me awake. "Welcome back! We were all so worried about you!" he said.

"Good evening. It's good to see you again, Dr. Chan," I replied, somewhat groggily.

"How did you recognize me?" he asked with obvious surprise on his face.

"Because I saw you," I told him. "Aren't you the one who removed the fluid from my lungs in the middle of the night because I was having difficulty breathing?"

He was visibly puzzled as he said, "Yes, but you were in a coma the whole time. Your eyes were closed!" He tried to dismiss it as he went on, "This is a really pleasant surprise! I didn't expect to see you awake, but I came to deliver some good news for your family. The test results for your liver and kidney function just came in and indicate that they're starting to function again." He looked very pleased.

"But I knew they were starting to function," I said blearily, feeling confused.

"You couldn't have known," Dr. Chan assured me patiently. "This was unexpected. Now get some rest," he instructed as he left the room.

My family was beaming, and looking more cheerful than I'd seen them in a long time. They thanked the doctor profusely for the good news as he went out.

After Dr. Chan was gone, I asked my husband, "Why was he so surprised that I recognized him? I saw him treating me. Wasn't he the doctor who told you my organs had already shut down, and that I wouldn't make it and only had a few hours to live?"

"How did you hear that?" Danny asked. "He didn't say that in this room. We had that conversation down the corridor, about 40 feet away!"

"I don't know how I heard it. And I don't understand why, but I already knew the test results of my organ function, even before the doctor came in," I said.

Although I was still very groggy, it was becoming apparent that something had definitely happened within me.

OVER THE FOLLOWING DAYS, I WAS SLOWLY ABLE TO TELL my family what had happened in the other realm, and I also described a lot of things that had taken place while I was in the coma. I was able to relay to my awestruck family, almost verbatim, some of the conversations that had occurred not only around me, but also outside the room, down the hall, and in the waiting areas of the hospital. I could describe many of the procedures I'd undergone, and I identified the doctors and nurses who'd performed them, to the surprise of everyone around.

I told the oncologist and my family how I'd had difficulty breathing and had begun to choke on my own fluid in the middle of the night, when my husband sounded the emergency alarm. I recounted how the nurses arrived and made an emergency call to the doctor, who came rushing in as everyone thought I was drawing my last breath. I described every detail of this incident, including what time it happened, much to everyone's shocked surprise.

I even identified the person who'd panicked when I was admitted. I told my family, "That's the nurse who said my veins had all retracted. He went on and on about how my limbs had no flesh and I was all bones, so it was going to be impossible to find a vein to start an intravenous flow—in fact, his tone sounded like it was pointless to even try to find my veins!"

My brother was upset by this piece of information and later admitted that he'd reprimanded the man, telling him: "My sister heard every word you said when you couldn't find her veins. She could tell that you were ready to give up on her."

"I had no idea she could hear me! She was in a coma!" The nurse was both surprised and shocked, and subsequently apologized to me profusely for his insensitivity.

WITHIN TWO DAYS OF COMING OUT of the coma, the doctors informed me that because my organs had miraculously started functioning again, the swelling caused by toxic buildup had subsided considerably. I was extremely positive and optimistic, requesting that the doctors remove the food tube because I was ready to eat independently. One of my oncologists protested, claiming that I was too malnourished and my body wasn't absorbing nutrients. But I insisted that I knew I was ready for food—after all, my organs were functioning normally again. She reluctantly agreed, saying that if I didn't eat properly, the device was going right back in again.

The food tube was possibly the most uncomfortable of all the ones connected to my body. It was inserted through my nose and traveled down the back of my trachea into my stomach. Liquid protein was fed through it directly into my digestive system. The presence of this tube made my throat feel parched and dry and the inside of my nose itchy and uncomfortable. I was impatient to get rid of it.

After the tube came out, the doctor suggested to my family that the best solid food for me right then was probably ice cream. Not only would it soothe the abrasions in my throat, it would be easy for me to digest without the added effort of needing to chew. My eyes lit up at the suggestion, and Danny set out to get me a tub of my favorite brand of chocolate ice cream.

When the other oncologist performed his routine checkup, he couldn't hide his surprise. "Your tumors have visibly shrunk—*considerably*—in just these three days!" he exclaimed incredulously. "And the swelling of all your glands has shrunk to almost half their previous size!"

The following day, to my delight, the oxygen tube came out. The doctors tested me and realized I was breathing without any aid, so they removed it. I was already sitting up in bed, although my head had to be propped up with pillows because I was too weak to hold it up for any length of time. I was still in really high spirits. I wanted to talk to my family, and I was especially excited to see Anoop and catch up with him.

By this point, I wanted to listen to my iPod, and I requested that Danny bring it to the hospital for me. Because of all the tubes and wires that were still plugged into me, plus the wound from the skin lesion on my neck, I couldn't wear the earphones. So Danny connected a little pair of speakers and put them on my bedside table so that I could listen to my music.

Because of my euphoric state, I continually wanted to listen to upbeat tunes, although I didn't have the strength in my muscles to even get out of bed, let alone dance. But in my head, I was bopping away happily, and the music helped contribute to my ecstatic mood. At the time, I didn't even fully understand why I was so positive—I just felt that I *knew* something.

I felt like a child. I wanted my music, I wanted to eat ice cream and talk to my family members, and I was laughing and happy. I couldn't get out of bed or move around, but everything seemed perfect in a way I'd never experienced before.

Since I was still in the ICU, the doctors decided that I was becoming disruptive to the other patients who were seriously ill! Their family members had started to complain about the music, laughter, and chatter that was coming from my side of the curtain.

"I don't know what to make of you!" Dr. Chan said when he came to see me during his morning rounds. "I don't even know what to write in your file. Your case is truly remarkable!"

So on my fifth day in the hospital, I was transferred to a regular room, where I had the privacy to listen to my music and laugh as much as I pleased!

SLOWLY—VERY SLOWLY IN FACT—THE UNDERSTANDING of what had happened was coming to me. As my mind cleared and I began to remember the details of what had taken place, I found myself wanting to cry about every little thing. There was a tinge of sadness at leaving behind the amazing beauty and freedom of the other realm. At the same time, I still found myself happy and grateful over being back and reconnecting with my family. I was crying tears of both regret and joy simultaneously.

In addition, I felt a bond with everyone in a way I never had before—not only all the members of my family, but every nurse, doctor, and orderly who came to my room. I had an outpouring of love for each person who came to do something for me or take care of me in any way. This wasn't a form of affection that I was familiar with. I felt as though I were connected to them all at a deep level and knew everything they were feeling and thinking, almost as though we shared the same mind.

My bed was next to the window, and shortly after being transferred into the room, one of the nurses asked me if I'd like to sit up and look outside. I realized that I hadn't seen the outside world for some time, so I felt excited by the prospect and said, "Yes, absolutely!"

The nurse propped me up, and the moment I looked out the window, my eyes welled up. I couldn't keep myself from crying. It hadn't registered until that moment that the hospital was located only a few blocks away from my childhood home in Happy Valley.

As I mentioned earlier, this wasn't where I'd been going to for my treatments and blood transfusions over the last few years, which was more like a large clinic than a full scale hospital. The day I went into a coma was the first time I entered the doors of this facility.

So there I was, looking at almost the very same view I had as a child. I could see the horse racetrack in front of the hospital building—and the tram line I'd ridden with Ah Fong! As I gazed teary eyed at the scenes of my childhood, I felt as though I'd come full circle.

Oh my God, I can't believe this, I thought in wonder. *Look at the trams, the park, the buildings from my childhood. What a message— I'm getting another chance! I can make a fresh start.*

Although the view was familiar to me and the scenery was ordinary, somehow the world looked brand-new. Everything seemed so fresh and sharp and beautiful, as though I were looking at it for the first time. The colors were brighter than I knew them to be, and I was noticing every detail as if for the first time. I looked at the surrounding buildings, one of which was the low-rise I grew up in; the park immediately across the street, which I visited when I was little; the trams trundling by; the cars driving past; the pedestrians walking along with their dogs or busily running errands. I saw everything with new eyes, as though I were a child again. The view couldn't have been more ordinary, yet it was the best I'd seen in a long time . . . maybe ever.

CHAPTER 10

Proof of Healing

Several days after coming out of the ICU, I started physical therapy to strengthen my muscles. The first day that I could walk across the room, a nurse took me into the bathroom so that I could see myself in the mirror. As I looked at my skeletal reflection, my heart sank. It was the first time since coming out of the coma that I felt disheartened.

I asked the nurse to leave me alone for a few minutes so that I could have some privacy. I just continued to gaze at myself in the mirror. I almost didn't know the person who looked back at me—almost couldn't recognize her. Most of my hair had fallen out in great clumps; my eyes seemed too big for their sockets; my cheekbones jutted out; and I had a bandage on the side of my neck below my right ear, hiding a huge, open skin lesion. I stood riveted by my own image, and I began to cry.

I wept not for the sake of my vanity. My physical appearance didn't seem important in that moment. Instead, I had the same deep sadness that anyone would feel when looking at a person in that condition. I felt sorrow combined with profound empathy. I could see in that image—in that face, in those eyes—the years of pain that it took to get where I was today, standing there in front of the mirror.

How could I have allowed myself to go through so much anguish? How could I cause myself this much pain? I grieved.

Yes, I felt as though I'd done it to myself. I reached my hand up toward the mirror, and as I touched the image of my tearful face, I made a promise that I'd never hurt myself so badly again.

THE DOCTORS WERE BEING CAUTIOUS ABOUT my healing, particularly because of the state I was in when I entered the hospital. They wanted to adjust the mix and dosage of the chemotherapy they were giving me—which, at one time, I'd greatly feared.

I watched as the nurses came in to administer the chemo. They hung the bag of drugs on the IV stand. Each bag, which they were feeding directly into my veins, was labeled "POISON" in huge, red capital letters. The nurses wore masks and latex gloves so that they couldn't accidentally have contact with any of the dangerous chemicals. Strangely, it seemed that it was acceptable for these drugs to be introduced directly into my bloodstream.

I knew I didn't need the chemo. The doctors were administering it for their own reasons, not mine, for I knew that I was invincible. Nothing could destroy me, not even poison injected directly into my veins—the very thing I'd feared for so many years! Interestingly, I didn't suffer from the normal side effects. My medical team was very surprised that I didn't have the usual nausea associated with the treatment.

I felt a level of victory. I'd so completely overcome my fear of everything—from dying to cancer to chemotherapy—that this proved to me that it had been the *fear* destroying me. I knew full well that if this had been before my experience in the other realm, the very sight of the word *poison* in giant red letters labeling a drug that was coursing through my veins, coupled with the nurses all wrapped up in protective gear to avoid contamination, would have sent enough fear through me to kill me. The psychological effect alone would have finished me, for I knew how fear-filled I was before.

But instead, I felt invincible. I knew that the decision to come back that I'd made on the other side completely overrode anything going on in the physical world.

The doctors wanted to conduct a range of tests to obtain a more accurate picture of my present situation and adjust the chemo dosage accordingly. I reluctantly agreed, mostly because I knew that they needed the tests more than I did as proof that I was healed, but also partly because I already knew what the results would be. It would give me a sense of victory to prove myself correct. However, the doctors felt that I was still too weak to withstand extensive testing, so they decided to spread the procedures over a couple of weeks while I continued to get stronger. I weighed less than 90 pounds, and I was required to get my nutrition levels up before any tests that involved even minor surgery, since any additional healing requirements might put a strain on my already-depleted resources.

My skin lesions were huge, gaping wounds that were being cleaned and dressed every day by the nursing staff. Because the lesions were both wide and deep, the doctors felt that they wouldn't heal without intervention. My body had neither the nutrition nor the strength required to recover from major injuries, so a reconstructive surgeon came to assess the situation.

He confirmed that my wounds were indeed too large to heal on their own, particularly since my body didn't have the nutrients necessary to support the process. However, he felt that I was still too frail to withstand reconstructive surgery and requested that the nurses continue to keep the lesions clean and dressed until I built up enough strength for the procedure. I still had barely any muscle or flesh on my bones.

ABOUT SIX DAYS AFTER COMING OUT OF the ICU, I began to feel a little bit stronger and was starting to walk up and down the hospital corridor for short periods of time before needing to rest. The first test that the doctors decided that I was strong enough to endure was a bone-marrow biopsy. This is a very painful procedure that consists of a thick needle being inserted into the base of the spine, to withdraw marrow from the bone.

It's common for advanced-stage lymphoma to metastasize to the bone marrow, so the doctors were expecting to see this confirmed in my test results. They intended to use these results to determine which drugs to put me on and what the dosage should be.

I recall the day I got the results. The doctor came into my room with a whole team of hospital personnel, looking concerned. Then he spoke: "We have the results of the bone-marrow biopsy, but it's a little disturbing."

For the first time in days, I felt some anxiety. "Why? What's the problem?"

My family members were in the hospital room with me, and all of them looked worried.

"We can't find the cancer in your bone-marrow biopsy," he said.

"So how is that a problem?" Danny asked. "Doesn't that just mean she doesn't have cancer in her bone marrow?"

"No, that's not possible," the doctor said. "She definitely has cancer in her body—it can't just disappear so quickly like that. We simply have to find it; and until we do, it's a problem, because I'm unable to determine her drug dose."

So the doctors then sent my bone-marrow sample to one of the most sophisticated pathology labs in the country. Four days later, the results returned negative—there was no trace of cancer. I felt an overwhelming sense of victory upon hearing the news.

Not to be defeated, the doctors then wanted to conduct a lymph-node biopsy to find the cancer. At first, my newfound sense of self made me want to retaliate and tell them, "No, you will *not* conduct any more tests, because it's my body, and I already *know* that you won't find *anything!*"

However, as the doctors continued to insist, reminding my family of the state I was in when I entered the hospital just a few short days prior, I decided to let them go ahead because I knew full well that they wouldn't find anything. I also realized that it would continue to bring me a sense of victory to trump every medical test they gave me.

I actually said to the doctor, "Do what you need to do, but I want you to know that you're all doing this to convince your-selves. I already know the results!"

They gave me another few days to build up some more strength for the lymph-node biopsy, which entailed minor surgery. Just prior to the procedure, I was sent down to the radiology department. The radiologist was to use ultrasound equipment to find the largest lymph node and mark the spot on my skin where the surgeon could make the incision for the biopsy.

As I lay there on the table in the radiology lab, I noticed that my earlier scans, taken the day I entered the hospital, were pinned up on the light box, showing where all the tumors were. The radiologist noted from those scans that my neck was ridden with swollen glands and tumors, so he ran the ultrasound machine along the back of my neck, up to the base of my skull. Then he moved it along the sides of my neck, and finally up and down the front of my neck. I noticed confusion and bewilderment building up on his face.

He went back to refer to the scans hanging on the light box, then returned to where I was lying on the table. He asked if he could use the ultrasound under my arms. I said okay, but after checking that area, he still looked bewildered. He then scanned my chest, back, and abdomen.

"Is everything okay?" I asked.

"I'm confused," he said.

"Why? What's wrong?" I was getting an inkling of what was happening.

"Excuse me for a minute," he answered.

The radiologist then went over to a telephone not far away, and I heard him calling my oncologist.

"I don't understand. I have scans that show this patient's lymphatic system was ridden with cancer just two weeks ago, but now I can't find a lymph node on her body large enough to even suggest cancer," I heard him say.

A smile broke across my face, and as he came back toward the table, I sat up and said, "Right, so I guess I can go now!"

"Not so fast," he responded. "Your oncologist *insists* that I find a lymph node to biopsy, because it's not possible that you have no cancer in your body. Cancer doesn't just disappear like that. So I'll have to identify a node in an easy to access location, like your neck."

He proceeded to mark a lymph node on my neck, even though it wasn't enlarged. I was then scheduled for surgery, and the surgeon made a small incision on the left side of my neck to remove one of my lymph nodes.

Because this was done under local anesthetic, I was fully conscious. I really disliked the discomforting sensations I felt on my neck as the doctor cut the lymph node. I still remember smelling my own burning flesh as the surgeon cauterized my wound. I thought that maybe agreeing to let them do this wasn't such a good idea after all!

However, once again, the results showed that there was no trace of cancer.

At this point, I really started to protest the continued tests and drugs, because deep down, I knew without a doubt that I was healed. I was also starting to get restless about being confined in the hospital. I wanted to get out and start exploring the world again, especially since I knew that I was going to be well. But the doctors resisted me, insisting I needed more tests and more drugs. They reminded me of the state I was in when I was admitted.

"If you can't find any cancer in my body, why do I still need this?" I asked them.

"Just because we can't find the cancer, doesn't mean it's not there. Don't forget, you were terminal when you came in just a few weeks ago!" they responded.

But finally, they gave me a full-body positron-emission tomography (PET) scan, and when the results showed that I was free from cancer, my treatment came to an end.

Also, to the amazement of the medical team, the arrangements they'd made with the reconstructive surgeon to close the lesions on my neck were unnecessary because the wounds healed by themselves.

ON MARCH 9, 2006, five weeks after entering the hospital, I was released to go home. I was able to walk unaided, although I still needed a little bit of help to go up or down stairs. But I was in such a high state of euphoria that the doctors actually wrote in big letters across my hospital discharge slip: "Discharged to go home for further rest. No shopping or partying for at least six weeks!"

But I wasn't having any of that! Just one week later, for my birthday on March 16, I went to my favorite restaurant, Jimmy's Kitchen, for dinner with my family to celebrate my new life. And the following week, on March 26, I attended a friend's wedding. Much to the shock of my friends who knew what I'd just gone through, I danced and drank champagne gleefully. I knew more than ever that life was to be lived with joy and abandon.

CHAPTER 11

"Lady, whichever way I look at it, you should be dead!"

Several weeks after I was given the all clear from cancer, I was still processing everything that had happened, trying to make sense of it. I was getting used to people I knew being visibly shocked when they saw me for the first time since I'd come out of the hospital.

Although no one ever said it to my face, I knew most of them had thought I was going to die when they last saw me. They never expected to see me again. Some tried to conceal their surprise at how healthy I'd become in such a short time, but others didn't hide it so well.

"Oh my God, is that you?" my yoga teacher said, her jaw almost hitting the floor when I walked into her studio for the first time in six months. "You look amazing! I heard you were getting better, but I never realized you were this well!"

Amirah had been my yoga instructor on and off for several years, and she was a lovely person with a beautiful studio that overlooked the Victorian part of Hong Kong's central business district. She'd been aware I was sick, and as I became weaker and was unable to do many of the poses, she worked with me gently or had me just lie in the shavasana pose (this consists of lying down in total relaxation, as though asleep). When I could no longer do any other posture except shavasana, I still attended Amirah's practice because I just loved to soak in the positive energy of the class.

Finally, when I couldn't go out and was confined to a wheelchair and connected to a portable oxygen tank while being cared for at home by a full-time nurse, I stopped going to Amirah's studio.

So as soon as I was well enough to go out on my own, I wanted to walk in during the middle of a class and surprise her—and she was certainly surprised! Amirah then introduced me to the people in the practice space, not all of whom knew me. But those who did remember me were equally shocked. One lady's eyes welled up as she recalled how sick I was in the last days I attended the class. She never thought she'd see me again, yet there I was . . . all she could say was that it was a miracle.

EVERYONE I MET WAS CURIOUS TO KNOW what had happened. How did I get so much better so quickly? But I found it was very difficult to explain, and I started to realize that I didn't fully understand it myself. I just couldn't find a way to describe what I'd gone through so that others could understand. The words for such an experience didn't seem to exist, especially in English.

Then one day I received an e-mail from Anoop with a link to a website about near-death experiences, or NDEs. He'd been researching to see if anyone else had gone through something similar to me, and he found the Near Death Experience Research Foundation's (NDERF) website, **www.nderf.org**. In his message, he said that what I experienced sounded similar to some of the experiences that people had shared on this website, and he wanted me to take a look.

I didn't know very much about near-death experiences. I'd heard of them, and maybe seen a documentary or two on TV, but I didn't know anyone who'd had one—and least of all did I ever expect to undergo one myself!

As I began to read the information on the website that my brother had sent me, I felt myself getting goose bumps as I discovered stories that shared some similarities with mine. None of them had the element of illness that I had, but some of what they experienced in the other realm was very similar. Several spoke of expansion, clarity, and a feeling of oneness—that we're all connected. They expressed feeling no judgment, only overwhelming, unconditional love. They talked of meeting departed loved ones or other beings who cared about them, and they had a sense of universal understanding and knowledge. I couldn't get over the fact that others had experienced that feeling of acceptance and unity, the knowledge that we're all universally cherished. Many of them shared that after their NDE, they felt a sense of purpose, and that was exactly how I felt!

After reading a few accounts, I noticed a banner on the site that said, "Have you had a near-death experience you would like to share? Click here!" So I did. A lengthy, highly detailed form popped up, and I started filling it out. I hadn't written down my experience before, only tried to talk about it with close friends and family members, so this was the first time I'd analyzed it in such detail.

Since this was the first time I was putting it all down for someone unfamiliar with my situation, I wanted to make sure I articulated what I wanted to say very clearly. The questions also made me think about parts of my experience in ways I never had before. I filled out all the details about having cancer, everything I experienced when I crossed over and then came back, and finally the cancer disappearing very rapidly. After completing the fields on the form and adding all the extra details in the spaces provided, I hit "submit." A message popped up, saying, "Thank you for sending us your testimony. We will contact you within the next three weeks to inform you whether your experience will be posted on our site."

By that time, it was late at night for me, so I went to bed thinking that I probably wouldn't hear from them for a while. However, to my pleasant surprise, there was already a message in my inbox from a Dr. Jeffrey Long when I awoke the following morning.

Dr. Long explained that he was an oncologist as well as the owner of the NDERF site where I'd submitted my experience, and he found my experience to be one of the most exceptional he'd read. He wanted to ask me some follow-up questions, particularly regarding my medical condition, because he was extremely intrigued by my rapid healing. He said that I articulated my experience particularly well, and he wanted to know more about my cancer, such as when was I diagnosed, the duration of my illness, and how long it took for the cancer to heal after my NDE.

I answered all his questions as best I could, and he responded again almost immediately. There was a genuine buoyancy to his response. He said he was very excited about my answers, and he thanked me for allowing him to post my experience. He said that it would be inspiring for tens of thousands of people across the world. He then posted my account with a direct link on the NDERF home page, including all the answers to his follow-up questions, which are still in the site archives today in the original format.

I subsequently found out that Dr. Long had printed out my submission as soon as he received it in order to read and reread it because he thought it was so remarkable, which he hadn't done with any other submission.

At the same time, my friend Peter Lloyd, who runs a publication called *Holistic Hong Kong,* was so amazed by what had happened to me that he asked permission to print my story. So I sent him an exact copy of what I'd submitted to the NDERF site, and he included it in his next issue.

Several weeks later, during the summer of 2006, I was contacted by another oncologist in the United States. His name was Dr. Peter Ko, and he said that he had a personal interest in studying spontaneous remissions. Within the space of three weeks, two different people had sent him the links to my experience, the one posted on the NDERF website and the other in *Holistic Hong Kong.* When he first received the NDERF link, Dr. Ko pretty much dismissed it as my submission was quite lengthy, and he receives many e-mails from people suggesting articles for him to read. But when he received the second e-mail, this time with a link to my story on *Holistic Hong Kong* with a note requesting that he read the article and telling him that he'd surely be interested, he decided to see what it was about.

After reading my story, he was so intrigued that he contacted Peter Lloyd and asked if there was some way of reaching me, since the website didn't give out my full name—it only identified my story as "Anita M's NDE." So Peter connected Dr. Ko and me via e-mail, and Dr. Ko immediately asked if he could call me because he had a lot of questions.

We spoke on the phone for several hours, and I gave him details of my experience and of my medical condition in particular. I then faxed him some of the pertinent pages of my medical history, including the doctor's report of February 2, the day I entered the hospital, describing my condition and prognosis, with the diagnosis "lymphoma, stage 4B."

After reading some of those pages, his first words were: "Lady, whichever way I look at it, you should be dead!"

Dr. Ko was so intrigued by my case that he arranged a business trip to Hong Kong so that he could go to the hospital where my experience took place and study my medical records.

It was mid-October when I met him in the hospital where I had my near-death experience. We sat in the lobby and spoke for a while, getting acquainted. He asked me questions about my experience and my illness, wanting to know everything from my perspective. Then we went to the administration office and asked for my records. They brought out this huge file, about three inches thick, and dropped it on the counter in front of us. We took it to the canteen, and Dr. Ko started to go through all the details page by page, pulling out pertinent documents to be copied.

I felt extremely excited and privileged to have two oncologists— first Dr. Long and now Dr. Ko—so interested in my experience. It validated my feelings that I'd come back for some greater purpose that was going to help others. I was grateful and delighted that my going through everything I did could perhaps assist someone else.

Dr. Ko asked me whether I would be open to speaking in public about what happened to me. He is, by his own admission, a skeptic by nature; but he was very excited by what he'd read in my hospital records and wanted to put his research on my case to good use immediately. He planned to organize a conference locally while he was still in Hong Kong in order to share his most recent findings with the medical community, and he wanted me to speak also. He told me that he'd already mentioned my case to several people in the local medical community, and had given a little bit of background about my story and my reluctance to accept conventional treatment.

Dr. Ko felt that it was important for the medical community to hear my story from my perspective. He said that he'd never come across a case of a full remission from such an advanced stage of cancer, let alone at such a rapid rate. He believed it was important for people to know about it. I was extremely excited to be asked and eager to share what had happened, so I agreed to speak at the conference.

I also put Dr. Ko in touch with our family general practitioner, Dr. Brian Walker, who confirmed that he'd been astounded by my recovery. Dr. Walker reiterated that he'd never seen such a rapid remission from such an advanced stage of cancer either. Dr. Ko spoke with Dr. Walker for some time about his observations of the progression of my cancer over the years, and Dr. Walker validated and endorsed many of the American physician's findings. Dr. Ko then contacted the press and made sure there was a reporter present at the conference to report my story in our local newspaper.

The following is an excerpt from the summary that Dr. Ko wrote up after his research through all my hospital records. He sent out this report, which I'm reproducing with his permission, as an e-mail to the press and medical community in connection with the conference. It recounts the details of my story from an oncologist's perspective, confirming my personal experience.

> I hope you find Anita's story compelling as I do . . . this encounter is turning out to be quite an eye-opener for me! When I came to HKG [Hong Kong] last month, my intention was to scrutinize her clinical history, and to either validate or invalidate her claims. Having satisfied myself with the factual details,

I actually find myself becoming more and more intrigued with her fantastic experience . . . especially the message she brought back! While clinical details can be a bit tedious for the general reader, I do want to provide them to you as reference, so that you can really appreciate how ill she was, and how dramatic a recovery she made. I hope that, plus a couple of personal observations, can put Anita's story on a more solid foundation:

1. A chronologic account of Anita's illness . . . In the Spring of 2002, she noticed a firm swelling just above her left collar bone. This was obviously an alarming sign to her physician. It was biopsied in April that year, and determined to be Hodgkin's Lymphoma. She was "staged" as 2A (early to mid/asymptomatic). You knew all about her reluctance to undergo conventional therapy, seeking a variety of alternative approaches. Her disease slowly progressed over the next 2½ years. By 2005, it began to interfere with her well-being. The cancer involved more and more of her lymph nodes, and became more and more enlarged. She also developed what we call "B symptoms" . . . night sweats, fever, skin itching, etc., all pointing to disease progression. She also developed pleural effusion (accumulation of fluid) on both sides of her chest, and throughout 2005, required several attempts to "tap the fluid" since it began to interfere with her breathing. By Xmas 2005, her course accelerated, and she began a downward spiral . . . the disease in her neck and chest wall was infiltrating the skin, resulting in large infected ulcers that would not heal. Unable to eat or absorb nourishment, weight loss, marked fatigue, muscle wasting . . . and her kidney functions started to be compromised.

The morning of February 2 found her unable to get out of bed; her entire face, neck, and left arm were swollen like a balloon. Her eyes were swollen shut . . . all due to compromised venous drainage from her head and neck, by massively enlarged and matted lymph nodes. She was gasping for breath as a result of massive pleural effusion bilaterally, despite using supplemental home oxygen. Feeling utterly helpless, her husband and mother called her family doctor for help, who urged them to get her to the hospital right away. There, an oncologist was alerted, and was shocked by the shape Anita was in. Another oncologist was summoned due to the difficult decisions she presented. Several other consultants were called in to address different failing organ-systems. The consensus was that she would not survive without intervention. While chemotherapy might be highly toxic in view of her multiple organ failure, it would be her only chance. During that night, she underwent multiple examinations with MRI and CT, had 2 liters of fluid tapped from her chest, started on 3 of 7 chemotherapy drugs*, and [was] placed in the ICU. This was when Anita drifted off into what she described as her NDE.

*The chemotherapy regimen called for 8 cycles of 7 drugs, each cycle taking three weeks.

2. Anita's dramatic recovery after she emerged from her NDE . . . The evening of Feb 3, Anita awoke, sat up, and declared to her family she would be okay. She conversed with the oncologist, who was baffled by her ability to even recognize him.

On Feb 4, Anita demanded to have her nasogastric tube removed, and promised her doctors she would eat what they brought her in order to gain some weight. She asked for her iPod to be brought from home.

On Feb 5, she greeted her doctors by asking them if they wanted to "join the party"; they eventually agreed to release her from the ICU on Feb 6.

By that time, much of her neck and facial swelling had resolved; the massively enlarged lymph nodes began to soften, and she was able to turn her head for the first time. The drugs for her first cycle were completed in mid-February. A plastic surgeon was asked to:

a. biopsy a lymph node on her neck, and

b. skin graft the large open sores on her neck and axilla.
   He could not find any lymph node on examination, and scheduled her for an ultrasound examination prior to the biopsy; he would also do the skin graft at the same time.

Three ultrasound exams failed to reveal any obviously pathologic lymph nodes. On Feb 27, he eventually biopsied one from her neck . . . and there was no evidence of cancer. The skin ulcers healed on their own without skin grafting.

The oncologists eventually agreed to let her go home on March 9, after her second cycle. She celebrated her birthday on March 16 at Jimmy's Kitchen, and went to a wedding, dancing and drinking champagne on March 26 . . . then began her third cycle. They all came to a compromise by doing a CT-PET scan after 6 cycles (July 24) . . . she was given a clean bill of health, and they stopped 2 cycles short.

Her recovery was certainly "remarkable." Based on my own experience and opinions of several colleagues, I am unable to attribute her dramatic recovery to her chemotherapy. Based on what we have learned about cancer cell behaviors, I speculate that something (non-physical . . . "information"?) either switched off the mutated genes from expressing, or signaled them to a programmed cell death. The exact mechanism is unknown to us, but not likely to be the result of cytotoxic drugs.

I think my encounter with Anita's experience shall set the stage for me to learn more about this phenomenon, and about the true nature of our selves!

The conference was attended by members of the medical profession, particularly professors from the oncology department of the local teaching hospital. In addition, there were a number of people there who'd been invited by myself, Dr. Ko, or some of the professors. Subsequently, Dr. Ko, Dr. Walker, and I were all invited to be interviewed on the radio about my case. (The newspaper article and radio interview are currently on my website: **www.anitamoorjani.com.**)

As a direct result of the conference and my meeting members of the medical faculty at the Hong Kong University, I was invited to be a consultant in their department of behavioral studies, speaking and advising the professors on the psychology of facing cancer and death. I was asked to speak to both the faculty and the students on a regular basis on this subject, and I enjoyed it tremendously.

Dr. Ko compiled a report of his medical findings from my file, along with his questions, and sent it to cancer institutes around the globe. To date, none of them have been able to answer his questions, and none of them have come across anyone on record who's had such a dramatic turnaround.

These are some of the unexplained phenomena that Dr. Ko shared with me that still remain a mystery:

— My medical records show that my organs had already shut down at the time I entered the hospital, yet something caused them to start functioning again. Dr. Ko is intrigued by what would cause their recovery. He also noticed a remark written by the oncologist saying: "patient's family have been informed," which Dr. Ko interpreted as the doctor making a note that my family had been notified that I was dying.

— My records confirmed that I had tumors the size of lemons throughout my body, from the base of my skull all around my neck, armpits, and chest, all the way down to my abdomen. But several days later, there was at least a 70 percent reduction in their size. He's curious as to how it was possible for billions of cancer cells to leave my body so quickly when the organs were failing.

— I had open skin lesions, and it's recorded in my file that they needed reconstructive surgery since my body didn't have the necessary nutrients to heal, because I was completely malnourished and my muscles were already wasted when I entered the hospital. The doctors' notes indicate that reconstructive surgery would be scheduled when I got stronger. Yet the wounds healed completely by themselves, well before the medical team was ready to operate.

These all come down to the main question that Dr. Ko and others want to understand about spontaneous remissions: *What flicked the switch, to turn the body around from dying to healing?*

As for my own situation, I know the answer . . . but it's not something that can be found in medicine.

CHAPTER 12

Seeing Life with New Eyes

For the first few months after coming out of the hospital, I felt euphoric, as though on a permanent high. Everything and everyone appeared beautiful, and there was magic and wonder in even the most mundane of objects or events. Take my living-room furniture, for example, which had been with us for many years without seeming special in any way. After returning home, I saw beauty in the woodwork that I'd never noticed before, and I was able to sense the labor that went into the construction. I felt wonder at being able to operate my car again (which I couldn't do in the last eight months of my cancer). I was in awe of my ability to coordinate my hands, eyes, and legs to drive through the streets. I was amazed by the human body and life itself.

As the months passed, I began to feel that I needed to do something with my life again. But as I thought of what I might want to do, I felt overwhelmed. I didn't know where to begin to pick up the pieces. The world wasn't the same place as the one I'd left behind. I'd spent the past four years dealing with being sick. During that time, my entire focus was on the disease. I'd spent years reading up, studying, and learning everything I possibly could about cancer. My entire purpose had revolved around my disease and trying to heal it. In a way, I'd begun to identify more with being someone who had cancer than with life. And now it was gone. What was I going to do with the rest of my life?

Prior to my diagnosis, I'd been fiercely independent. However, during the time I was sick, I was completely reliant on Danny and my other family members. Once I was well and back on my feet, everyone resumed their respective roles. Danny returned to work, my mother and brother flew back home, and I was left to figure out what I wanted to do with myself.

I couldn't imagine going back to being a relocation officer. I'd left my job shortly after being diagnosed, and had even interviewed my replacement. I hadn't been working for the last four years, as I was immersed in dealing with having cancer. Thinking about going back to work now felt different, and I realized *I* was different.

I felt as though I couldn't relate to anyone around me—or more accurately, that others couldn't relate to me. If I thought about going back to work, I couldn't figure out what I wanted to do. Nothing felt right anymore. I felt as though I didn't fit in with the people of this planet and their values. My priorities had changed, and I found that I was no longer interested in working in an office, reporting to anyone, or earning money for its own sake. I didn't care to network, go out with friends after work to unwind, deal with morning or evening rush hours, or commute to work in the city. And so for the first time since my NDE, I felt lost . . . and lonely.

IT BECAME INCREASINGLY DIFFICULT FOR ME to engage in conversations about everyday events. My attention span seemed to have shortened, and I found my mind wandering off on various tangents, even while talking with friends. I completely lost interest in what was going on in the world of politics and news, and even what my friends were doing. Yet I was riveted by the sun setting over the horizon while I sat on the beach enjoying an ice-cream cone, as though I were experiencing the loveliness of this world for the first time. The beauty of the sunset's orange glow reflecting on the water as I felt the wet sand under my feet and between my toes filled me with awe in a way it never had before. The tantalizing taste of creamy Belgian chocolate ice cream on my taste buds made me feel as though it was the first time I was having ice cream!

I saw divinity in everything—every animal and insect. I developed a much greater interest in the natural world than I had before. I couldn't even kill the mosquitoes that came buzzing around me. They were life forms and needed to be respected as such. They had a purpose. I didn't know what that was; I just knew they had one, as I did.

Each morning, I woke up wanting to explore the world anew. Every day was a fresh adventure. I wanted to walk, drive, explore, sit on the hills and the sand, and just take in this life! I was also deeply interested in the urban environment, and reconnected with it as though it were all new. I spent my time exploring markets, enjoying city views and the beautiful skyline of neon-lit skyscrapers, admiring our highly efficient public transportation system and the incredible suspension bridges that stretched across the water to connect the various islands that make up Hong Kong. I was awed by it all.

The deliciousness of each day made me feel as though I'd just been born. It was as if I'd entered the world as an adult, as if I'd been born for the first time on February 3, 2006.

At the same time, I found myself unable to reconnect with many of my old friends, whom I attempted to meet over lunch or coffee. Everyone was anxious to catch up with me, but most didn't understand how deeply and profoundly this experience had changed me. I found that I got restless and impatient in social situations. I couldn't sit still for long periods of time or engage in conversation about mundane routines.

I felt that people had lost the ability to see the magic of life. They didn't share my wonder or enthusiasm for my surroundings—and just being alive. They seemed caught up in routine, and their minds were on the next thing they had to do. It was exactly what I used to do before my NDE. Everyone was so caught up with doing that they'd all forgotten how to just be in the moment.

But most of all, I felt that I was at the edge of something wonderful that was about to unfold. I felt that there was some greater purpose to having experienced everything I'd just been through. Even with this inner excitement, however, with this feeling that I was on the precipice of some great adventure, I still didn't feel that I had to *do* or *pursue* anything for it to happen. *I just had to be myself, fearlessly!* In that way, I'd be allowing myself to be an instrument of love. I understood that this was the best thing that any of us could possibly do or be, for both the planet and ourselves.

Since I realized this, problems just didn't seem that big anymore. I felt that people were taking life and their problems too seriously—which is what I used to do. In the past, I was drawn into other people's dramas, as well as my own. But following my NDE, I just felt blessed to be alive and to get a second opportunity to express myself here. I no longer wanted to waste even one minute of the great adventure. I wanted to be as much *me* as I could possibly be and savor and taste every delicious minute of being alive!

I really didn't want to get bogged down with all the mundane, minor problems and issues such as worrying about the future, money, work, or household and domestic issues. All these things seemed so minor somehow, especially because I trusted in the process that I could feel was unfolding before me.

It seemed important to have fun and laugh. I felt a lightness that was completely new, and I laughed easily. I enjoyed the company of those who wanted to do the same.

WHENEVER I HAD CONVERSATIONS about illness, politics, or death, my views were so radically different because of my experience that I simply couldn't involve myself in the topics. I began to realize that my ability to judge and discern had become "impaired." I was no longer able to draw definite distinctions between what was good or bad, right or wrong, because I wasn't judged for anything during my NDE. There was only compassion, and the love was unconditional. I still felt that way toward myself and everyone around me.

So I found myself with nothing but compassion for all the criminals and terrorists in the world, as well as their victims. I understood in a way I never had before that for people to commit such acts, they must really be full of confusion, frustration, pain, and self-hatred. A self-actualized and happy individual would *never* carry out such deeds! People who cherish themselves are a joy to be around, and they only share their love unconditionally. In order to be capable of such crimes, someone had to be (emotionally) diseased—in fact, much like having cancer.

However, I saw that those who have this particular type of "mental" cancer are treated with contempt in our society, with little chance of receiving any practical help for their condition, which only reinforces their condition. By treating them in this way, we only allow the "cancer" in our society to grow. I could see that we haven't created a society that promotes both mental and physical healing.

This all meant that I was no longer able to view the world in terms of "us" and "them"—that is, victims and perpetrators. There's no "them"; it's all "us." We're all One, products of our own creation, of all our thoughts, actions, and beliefs. Even perpetrators are victims of their own self-hatred and pain.

I no longer viewed death in the same way as others did, either, so it was very hard for me to mourn anyone. Of course, if someone close to me passed on, I was sad because I missed them. But I no longer mourned for the deceased, because I knew they'd transcended to another realm, and I knew that they were happy! It's not possible to be sad there. At the same time, I also knew that even their death was perfect, and everything would unfold in the way it was meant to in the greater tapestry.

Because of my radically changed views, I became cautious about expressing my opinions, as I didn't want to be misunderstood. I knew it would be hard for others to understand concepts such as there being no judgment after we die, even for the worst of terrorists. Even for them, I perceived only compassion, total understanding, and clarity for why they acted out in the way they did. On a more mundane and down-to-earth level, I also knew that there wasn't going to be any judgment waiting for me in the afterlife if I chose not to follow religious or cultural dogma that didn't feel right for me.

So, slowly, I found myself seeking mainly my own company, unless I was with Danny. I felt safe with him. I knew he wouldn't judge me. My husband had been with me through my entire journey, and he was one of the very few who understood me. He listened patiently as I talked about my feelings and thoughts, and he helped me figure out all the new emotions.

I constantly felt a need to talk about my experience, to try to make sense of what happened, to unravel it, so Danny encouraged me to write in order to get my feelings out. I began writing and kept at it continually. I wrote on forums and blogs, and I found it to be very therapeutic as I moved forward in this new world.

CHAPTER 13

Finding My Path

I now held a view of life that very few, if any, in my social circle shared or even related to. And I was no longer afraid of anything. I didn't fear illness, aging, death, loss of money, or anything. When death holds no horror, there isn't much else left to be afraid of because it's always considered the worst-case scenario. And if the worst doesn't faze you, then what else is left?

I was also finding it challenging to integrate back into life because this world still didn't seem real to me. The other realm felt more genuine. And as I've described, I found myself grappling with how seriously everyone was taking everything—for example, how stressed out everyone was about money and finances, even though they had a lot of other beautiful things to enjoy and be thankful for. I also couldn't understand how much people neglected everything else—including love, relationships, talent, creativity, individuality, and so on—for the sake of money, and how much time they spent working at jobs they didn't enjoy. The way everyone viewed life seemed all wrong to me. Priorities and values were misaligned, and everything seemed back to front. I realized that I probably used to think that way, too, yet I couldn't imagine going back to it ever again.

I know I'll never again take on a job I don't enjoy just for the money, I found myself thinking. *My criteria for work and for doing things in general are so different now. My life and my time here are much more valuable to me.*

Danny found that after the intensity of seeing me through cancer and nearly dying, things weren't the same for him, either. Before my illness, he'd been working in sales and marketing for a multinational organization, and was responsible for Asian distribution. Going to work now felt uninspiring and monotonous after everything we'd been through together. We'd both grown, changed, and learned so much!

Danny had always dreamed of running his own business, and it was at this point that I told him to do it. I encouraged him to live his dream. Before my NDE, I would have been too afraid to encourage him, thinking only that it was a big risk; and if we failed, then how would we support ourselves?

But my views had changed, and fulfilling his dream seemed more important, as well as not living a life of regrets. So I encouraged him to set up the business he'd always wanted, developing and providing career assessment tools for students and corporations.

As things worked out, the shift from working for someone else to working for himself was made even easier when he was let go from his job for being away from work so much while he tended to me during my illness. In the past, this would have been a major upset. But after my NDE, it was just another way of seeing the universe working on our behalf. It was an opportunity to do something more exciting!

To pull off this new adventure, we had to downsize dramatically. We moved to a smaller home and cut back on a lot of our personal expenses. We ended up in a very humble neighborhood located a fair distance away from Hong Kong's bustling urban areas. Our home was in a remote village close to the China border, where we were isolated from our community, and this gave us an opportunity to regroup and reevaluate our lives. It was a drastic change from what we were used to, and it felt as though we were starting life afresh—a new beginning.

ONCE, I WOULD HAVE VIEWED THE LOSS of Danny's job or our needing to downsize dramatically and move out of the city as something negative or adverse. It would have caused a lot of fear because it threatened my security. However, because the words *Go back and live your life fearlessly!* kept reverberating in my head, I knew that everything was going to be fine. Out of the many messages I brought back from my NDE—we are all one, we are love at our core, we are magnificent—this was the strongest one and kept reverberating within me. Because it seemed to come from both my father and my best friend, Soni, whenever I hear it in my head, I hear it in the voice of either one or the other, depending on the situation. In this case, I saw the events all as part of a greater adventure that was unfolding, which gave me the feeling of starting life with a clean slate.

In addition, because of my NDE, I went from an outside-in view of reality to an inside-out view. That is, I used to think that the external world was real and that I had to work within its confines. This is pretty much how most people think. With this view, I gave my power to the world outside, and external events had the ability to control me—my behavior, moods, and thinking. Emotional reactions and feelings weren't considered real because they weren't tangible. They're thought to be merely reactions to external events. In that model, I was a victim of circumstances rather than the creator of my life. Even illness was an external event that just "happened" to me randomly.

However, after my NDE, I began to see myself as a divine and integral part of the greater Whole. This includes everything in the entire universe, everything that has ever existed and ever will, and it's all connected. I realized that I was at the center of this universe, and knew that we all express from our perspective, as we're each at the center of this great cosmic web.

Over time, as Danny and I built this new phase of our lives together, I understood these truths even more concretely. Although everything exists within this web of interconnection and we have access to it all, my world at any point in time is a tapestry made up of all my thoughts, feelings, experiences, relationships, emotions, and events up to that point. Nothing exists for me until it's brought into my tapestry. And I can increase or limit it by expanding my experiences and awareness or restricting them. I feel as though I have a certain amount of choice about what I allow into my observation.

When something comes into my awareness, it becomes a part of my tapestry. To refer back to the warehouse analogy, I've shone my flashlight on it. This means that it becomes part of my belief system—my truth.

I knew that the purpose of my life was to expand my tapestry and allow more and greater experiences into my life. So I found myself trying to stretch the limits of what was considered possible in all the areas where I'd previously perceived limitations. I started to question what things we all presumed to be true but were, in fact, just socially determined beliefs. I looked at everything I judged to be negative or impossible in the past and questioned it, particularly beliefs that triggered feelings of fear or inadequacy within me.

Why do I believe this? I asked myself. *Is it purely cultural and social conditioning? It might have applied to me at some point, but does it still hold true? Does it serve me to continue to believe a lot of what I was brought up and taught to think?*

In some situations, maybe, but in a lot of cases, the answer was a definite *no.*

I was brought up to believe that women should be submissive. There was always a level of judgment toward those who were overly assertive or forceful or who held high position, because a woman's primary role was to be a supportive wife and mother. I never met this standard.

I'd spent a lifetime judging myself, beating myself up for not meeting these expectations. I always felt inadequate. But following my NDE, I understood that these were a false set of socially determined standards.

I also used to believe that I wasn't spiritual enough and needed to work harder in that area. Then I discovered that we're all spiritual, regardless of what we do or believe. We can't be anything else, because that's who we are—spiritual beings. We just don't always realize it, that's all.

I understood that true joy and happiness could only be found by loving myself, going inward, following my heart, and doing what brought me joy. I discovered that when my life seems directionless and I feel lost (which still happens to me frequently), what it really means is that I've lost my sense of self. I'm not connected with who I truly am and what I've come here to be. This has tended to happen when I stop listening to my own internal voice and give my power away to external sources, such as TV commercials, newspapers, big drug companies, my peers, cultural and societal beliefs, and the like.

Previously when I felt lost, one of the first things I did was to search *outside* for answers. I looked to books, teachers, and gurus, in the hope that they'd provide me with the ever-elusive solution. That's exactly what I did when I was first diagnosed with cancer. But I only ended up feeling even more adrift because I was giving my own power away again and again.

I FOUND THAT HAVING AN INSIDE-OUT VIEW MEANS being able to fully trust my inner guidance. It's as though what I feel has an impact on my entire universe. In other words, because I'm at the center of my cosmic web, the Whole is affected by me. So as far as I'm concerned, if I'm happy, the universe is happy. If I love myself, everyone else will love me. If I'm at peace, all of creation is peaceful, and so on.

If things seemed challenging, instead of trying to change them physically (which is what I did pre-NDE), I began checking in with my internal world. If I'm stressed, anxious, unhappy, or something similar, I go inward and tend to that first. I sit with myself, walk in nature, or listen to music until I get to a centered place where I feel calm and collected. I noticed that when I do so, my external world also changes, and many of the obstacles just fall away without my actually doing anything.

What I mean by being "centered" is experiencing being at the center of my cosmic web, being *aware* of my position. This is really the only place any of us ever are, and it's important to *feel* our *centrality* at the core of it.

But from time to time, I forgot my central place in the cosmos. I got caught up in all the dramas, contradictions, angst, and pain of the physical world and couldn't see myself as one of the expanded, magnificent, infinite beings we all truly are.

Luckily, I realized at those times that we never really become disconnected from the center. Rather, we temporarily lose sight of it and don't feel the sense of peace and joy that comes from it. We get caught up in the illusion of separation and can't see that happiness and sadness go hand in hand—like light and dark, yin and yang. Our sense of disconnection is simply part of the illusion of duality that makes it difficult to see oneness forming out of perceived separation. But getting centered means seeing through this and once again *feeling* our infinite place at the *center of it all* . . . at the *center of oneness.*

I still had the visceral knowledge that we're all one with the universe. Therefore, I knew that even while I'm in my physical body, whether I'm aware of it or not, *I am* at the center of the great cosmic web that is the universe! This is the same as realizing my magnificence and my connection to the Infinite.

As the months turned into years, I've put all this awareness into practice more and more. Sometimes, when I had a lot to do and things were stressful, I was accused of wasting time if I took a break to get centered. But if I tried to resolve things purely on the physical level, I knew it would be slow going. To this day, it still feels like walking through molasses, and dealing with issues only in this way causes me great frustration and increases my stress levels.

However, I discovered that if I take time out and reclaim my center, regardless of what people around me think, many of the primary stumbling blocks disappear once I'm aware of my connection to the Whole and feeling calm and happy. I receive a lot of clarity during those sessions, and purely by staying centered, many of the remaining challenges just fall away. I've found this to be a much more effective way of dealing with my life than solely dealing with it from the external. This is a direct result of my NDE and comes from knowing that I'm a part of a great cosmic tapestry, and that I'm at the center of it and can get in touch with the whole universe by turning inward.

Over the years since my NDE, I've experienced changes in my external requirements, too. I've discovered that I need to be near nature, particularly the sea, in order to feel my best. Similar to the wonder I felt in my first days out of the hospital, I find that I can instantly connect with my NDE state by looking at the waves and listening to the ocean.

I've watched in delight as the friends I've become close to and my immediate family members have made shifts of their own. And this may sound unusual, but since my NDE, many people have told me that they feel an energy change when they're around me. I rarely speak about this publicly because I believe that such things come from within the self. I may be merely reflecting to them what they were ready to experience.

Because of my experience, I absolutely do strongly believe that we *all* have the capacity to heal ourselves as well as facilitate the healing of others. When we get in touch with that infinite place within us where we are Whole, then illness can't remain in the body. And because we're all connected, there's no reason why one person's state of wellness can't touch others, elevating them and triggering their recovery. And when we heal others, we also heal ourselves and the planet. There's no separation except in our own minds.

MY LIFE HAS HAD ITS UPS AND DOWNS, and there are times when I feel I have to really work hard at being centered. I have to handle mundane things such as household chores and paying the bills, and since my NDE, I have trouble focusing down on those details. However, I'm never far away from finding my place in the universe again and feeling those words in my soul: *Go out and live your life fearlessly!*

I've also found that although I have made some new friends— including one in particular who's really helped me understand and process my experience—I seem to have difficulty reconnecting with many of my old ones. I'm not as social as I was in the past, and I don't enjoy the same things. I had a lot of friends before, but now I only let a very, very few people into my private life, many of whom I met through an NDE group over the last few years. A handful of us have become very close, and some of them have had similar experiences of their own.

I'm also still devoted to my immediate family members—my husband, mother, and brother. They were with me right through my crisis and my hours of need, and I feel very attached to them. It's become difficult for me to feel that close to others.

It's not that I try to be a loner. I still reach out, and I really enjoy helping people gain greater understanding, which I do through my writing and my current work as a cultural trainer. And as you'll see in the next chapter, the act of allowing and being myself has had a huge impact for me in this great adventure.

CHAPTER 14

Healing Is Only the Beginning

The book that you're holding is proof of what happened when I put the act of allowing to work. I want to share with you the series of synchronicities that had to take place for this book to come into existence.

Immediately after my NDE and healing, I was euphoric and wanted to shout out what I knew from the rooftops! I wanted everyone to know about what had happened to me and to feel what I was feeling. Yet at the same time, I felt trepidation about sharing it openly and taking any overt action toward publicizing my story or garnering attention. I simply didn't feel prepared to deal with all the attention and scrutiny I sensed it would attract.

Since yin always seems to combine with yang in the cycle of life, I found that although I was somewhat concerned about how my experience would be received, something still told me that I needed to share it with a much wider audience. There was both the desire to talk about it and the need to pull back. I knew that when the time was right—and when I felt ready within myself—the way to greater attention and exposure would unfold with the ease I'd sensed during my NDE.

In the meantime, I simply followed the understanding I gained from my experience as I described in the previous chapter. I stayed true to myself and went about the business of living in the way that made me the happiest—following my bliss, as it were. I felt certain that those who were ready or needed to hear what I had to say would find me. I remained open at all times to all possibilities regarding how far my message would spread of its own accord. Basically, I have always been in a state of allowing when it comes to this subject, but nothing prepared me for what was to unfold. . . .

IN MARCH 2011, I WAS IN THE UNITED ARAB EMIRATES, visiting my close childhood friend Sunita, who'd just opened a holistic training center there. She'd invited me to come and share my story with an audience in Dubai, and I was in very good spirits, as it had gone extremely well. I'd been unsure about how I'd be received and was pleasantly surprised. In fact, the visit seemed to trigger an internal shift that opened me up to feeling ready, finally, to share my story with the greater world.

For the first time since my NDE, I felt a transformation in the room where I was speaking—but the shift was really within me, even though it affected everyone present. I was in awe of the healing taking place before me. People were getting what they needed out of my experience, and everyone felt something happening in a very powerful way.

I recognized once again that others needed to know what I'd experienced! I realized that I had started to lose touch and hadn't been letting this *true me* flow. Once more, I'd been hiding my real self out of fear and trepidation. So it was there in Dubai that I felt in touch with my expanded, magnificent self again. I was ready to take on whatever life was going to deal me. In that room, I dropped all my inhibitions about sharing my experience with the world, even though I had no idea how I was going to be received. I was willing to take on the unknown and trust in the ambiguity.

Up until that point, I'd thought that the NDE was special just to me, and although I'd brought back a message to share with others, the healing mainly seemed to benefit *me*. This was part of the reason for my trepidation in sharing my story—I wasn't fully aware of how others were going to benefit from my experience. However, in that room that day, something shifted. As I watched the reaction of the others and the transformation that was taking place, I suddenly realized that both my getting cancer and my healing were actually *for the planet*. If we're all One, what happens to me, happens to all. And what happens *for* me also happens *for* the whole universe. I understood that the reason I even got sick and then chose to come back was to serve as an instrument for healing to take place in others—not just physical healing, but more important, emotional healing, since our feelings are actually what drive our physical reality.

Previously, I'd also thought that my healing from cancer was the culmination of my journey—it seemed to be the pinnacle of everything that had happened in my life and the end of my story. But I understood in Dubai that my recovery was just the beginning. It was the opening of a new chapter of greater unfolding, and all I had to do was step into the ambiguity.

Again, I knew I wouldn't have to do anything; it would just unfold as long as I *allowed* it to happen. And in that moment, I thought, *Bring it on! Whatever you have in store for me, I'm open to it! Now I understand!*

I'D BEEN IN DUBAI A WEEK WHEN I WOKE UP ON MARCH 16 and checked my e-mail, expecting birthday wishes from my friends and family members. To my amazement, there was a message from an editorial assistant at Hay House, saying: "Wayne Dyer became a huge fan of yours after reading about your near-death experience. If you are interested in writing a book about your experience, Hay House would be very interested in working with you in developing and publishing it."

As I read those words, I couldn't stop tears from streaming down my cheeks. What an absolutely incredible birthday surprise! What a confirmation of my feelings the previous day!

I'd already been writing a book and had even given some thought as to how to get it published, but the enterprise seemed daunting and way beyond my capacity to achieve. And until just the day before, I hadn't been fully prepared to extend my outreach to the greater world.

Still, over the previous months, many people had asked me whether I was writing a book on my near-death experience. When I answered yes, they asked if I'd found a publisher yet, and I said no.

Most then told me: "Even though your story is amazing, it's really tough getting a publisher to even read a manuscript these days. There's so much of this kind of spiritual stuff out there now, so they probably wouldn't look at it. Be prepared to be turned down over and over again."

I also heard: "You need a literary agent to just get the manuscript onto the publisher's desk. They won't even look at something that doesn't come through a literary agent," and "You'd better self-publish. That's a lot easier!"

To each and every one of these individuals, I replied, "I actually don't plan to go banging on publishers' doors, or begging people to take my book. My story will spread at the rate it's meant to, and if it's supposed to reach the masses, the universe will conspire to make it happen."

At that point, I'd also mentioned to several friends that of all the options out there, I dreamed of one day being published by Hay House, because I thought they were the best for this genre, and I loved all their authors. I checked their website and found that they wouldn't accept manuscripts that didn't come through a literary agent. I didn't know how to even begin looking for an agent, so I just let it go and got on with my life.

As I explained earlier, since my NDE, I'd sensed that something big was going on. I felt guided and directed, even in those moments when my life didn't seem to be heading in any particular direction. I still trusted what I'd felt during my experience and knew that all was well and as it should be. Receiving the e-mail from Hay House confirmed that what I'd been feeling all along was exactly right.

Of course, I responded excitedly, saying, *"Yes, yes, yes!"* I even told the editorial assistant that it was my birthday, and what a lovely present this was!

SOME DAYS LATER, WHEN I WAS BACK at home in Hong Kong, I received a message from my old friend Veronica Lee, telling me that she'd been listening to Wayne Dyer's radio show when he spoke about me and my NDE. She said that he'd talked about me several weeks in a row, so I went to the Hay House Radio website, accessed the archives, and started listening. Lo and behold, there Wayne was, talking about my experience week after week! Of course, I was thrilled to hear him speak about me to such a wide audience.

Not long after this, I wanted to surprise Wayne and decided to call his show while he was broadcasting live, accepting callers and answering their questions. Because of the time difference, his program is broadcast at 4:00 A.M. Hong Kong time. So I set my alarm for 3:30, got up, tuned in online, and started dialing. On the first couple of attempts, the line was busy; but to my delight, I finally got through—and it wasn't even four o'clock yet.

The person who answered the phone asked my name, and where I was calling from. I was then put on hold. When the show actually started, after all the introduction and so on, Wayne's producer, Diane Ray, said, "Oh look, there's a caller from Hong Kong. Why don't we take that one?" My heart skipped a beat when I heard her say that. (I later learned that it's extremely difficult to get through to Wayne's radio show.)

Even before I came on the line, Wayne said, "Oh my God, I think I know who that must be! Is it who I think it is?"

"Hi, this is Anita," I replied.

"Oh my God, it's Anita, who had the NDE! I am so thrilled to have you on my show!" he exclaimed. "Diane, can you hold off on all the other calls? I'm going to spend the rest of the show on this one!" He then asked me to share my story on air.

After the show finished, Wayne asked me to stay on the line. We spoke some more, and he told me that he'd be honored to write the Foreword to my book, if I would let him.

I thought, *Let him—are you kidding? I'd be* <u>*thrilled!*</u>

Wayne then went on to tell me that he'd printed out my entire online NDE story, which is about 21 pages. He'd made about 40 copies and had been distributing them to everyone he knew. He'd shared it with his mother, and she'd drawn a lot of comfort from it. He also told me that he'd quoted me several times throughout his latest book, *Wishes Fulfilled.*

All I could think was, *Is this really happening? Wayne Dyer quoted <u>me</u> throughout his latest book?*

We then exchanged contact information, and Wayne told me that I was welcome to call him anytime.

I was filled with joy! I spent the next few days walking on air, unable to eat or sleep, with a constant feeling of butterflies in my chest. I'd felt that I was at the edge of something really big, and I knew this was going to be a challenging test of my ability to just hang tight and do nothing but be myself, enjoy the ride, and allow.

Over the next few weeks, I had many opportunities to speak with Wayne over the phone as we discussed the book and its direction, and he read me the beautiful Foreword he'd written, which brought me to tears once again. I'm a bit soft about these things— especially when seeing the vision from my NDE unfold before me.

During one of our conversations, Wayne told me that when he first read of my experience, he didn't *ask* Hay House to locate me. He *told* them that they *must* find me, and if I was writing a book, that they *must* publish it!

As you can imagine, I was blown away by this revelation, and I asked how he came to learn of my experience. He told me that he'd heard of me through a woman named Mira Kelley who lives in New York, and he then introduced us via e-mail. Mira and I began corresponding and speaking on the phone, and she told me of all the incredible little events that had to take place at precisely the right time for Wayne to have had access to my NDE. He doesn't surf online, nor does he enjoy spending any significant length of time on the computer reading long articles, so he wouldn't have stumbled on my story by accident.

I'll let Mira tell you the chain of events in her own words:

> On January 11, 2011, I spoke with a friend who told me that Wayne Dyer was leading a group of people through Europe on a tour called "Experiencing the Miraculous." My intuition

anchored on the word *miraculous*. I knew that Wayne had leukemia, and hearing this word somehow caused me to understand that he was ready for a miracle.

I initially talked myself out of contacting Wayne, but the feeling that I needed to speak with him persisted and became even more compelling. I assured myself that if I'm meant to be a tool in the hands of God, I have to allow for the unfolding of whatever miracles need to take place. Several days later, I wrote Wayne a letter.

When he called me about a month later, I'd forgotten about the incident. We spoke briefly and were about to hang up when I interrupted Wayne's good-bye. To my own surprise, I said that there was something I wanted to send him, something that he needed to read. Without a moment's pause, he gave me a fax number.

That "something" was Anita's NDE story, which had come to my inbox just the day before via a list of people who e-mail each other on spiritual topics. The person who sent the message pointed out the section of the story that spoke of all time existing simultaneously, which caught my eye because of my regression work; and reading Anita's account made me feel that magical sense of locking into the true vibration of my spirit.

The moment Wayne and I hung up, that question *Why?* crept up again. *Why did I feel so compelled to share Anita's story with Wayne?*

The only explanation I could think of back then was that it described so perfectly what I believed in and what I could offer. Through sending him Anita's story, I was saying: "I know you can be healed instantaneously. That possibility exists, and if you choose to know yourself as perfect health, I can assist you in creating that reality." It would have taken a lot longer conversation for me to say what Anita so simply and eloquently put into words.

Now I see a second reason. I understand that I'm part of the process that seeks to bring Anita's inspiring words to the entire planet. The timing was absolutely synchronous. Had that e-mail arrived any sooner, it wouldn't have been at the forefront of my thoughts, and I wouldn't have shared it with Wayne. Had it come later, it wouldn't be receiving this enormous recognition.

The synchronicity of this coming together so magically reminds us that everything happens at once, at the same timeless moment, just as Anita found during her NDE.

Wayne and I agreed to do a regression, and I flew out to Maui to meet with him. On April 15, when I went to Wayne's home, he was on the phone. When he hung up, he told me that he was speaking with Hay House and that they would publish Anita's book. His enthusiasm told me that he was ready for a miraculous event of his own. His session was profoundly powerful, and I share in his belief that he's healed of leukemia.

I went back to the message that brought Anita's story to me and found that it came from someone I didn't know—Ozgian Zulchefil, an engineer who lives in Constanta, Romania. When I shared the awe-inspiring synchronicities that he was part of, he responded that he was glad and joyful that I took the time to tell him, even though he doesn't remember where he found the account of Anita's NDE. He said that this serves as a confirmation that we constantly affect one another by what we do and say, even if we aren't aware of it. Therefore, he concluded, it's "important to have a really good, positive attitude for every moment of your life even if you don't see a reason for doing it in the first place." I couldn't help but smile.

Just a few days ago, I received an e-mail suggesting that I watch an inspiring interview with a woman named Anita Moorjani, who was miraculously healed of cancer following an NDE. A surge of excitement went through me as I recalled how Wayne and I had agreed that the two of us coming together allowed Anita's powerful words of love to affect and uplift millions of people. Receiving that e-mail confirmed that the circle has been completed. Simultaneously, Anita's words assisted in creating Wayne's healing.

By allowing Spirit to move through me, I became a tool in the hands of God in ways I could have never imagined.

Mira's story only reinforces that we're all—every single one of us—unique, indispensable facets of the infinite universe. Each of us is an integral part of the greater unfolding tapestry that's continually working toward healing the planet. Our only obligation is to always be true to ourselves and to allow.

As I look back on the trajectory of my life, it's crystal clear that every step along my path—both before and after my NDE, both those events I saw as positive and those I perceived as negative—has ultimately been to my benefit and guided me to where I am today. What's also very clear is that the universe *only* gives me what I'm ready for, and only *when* I'm ready. My trepidation about publicity slowed down the process, and when that anxiety was removed, I received the confirmation from the universe immediately through the Hay House e-mail. *I allow how much of what I want to come into my life . . . or not!*

The book you're reading is, from my perspective, just the latest proof of this. Had it not been for the environment I grew up in and the way I saw myself and reacted as I experienced all that transpired in my life, I might very well not have gotten cancer. Without the cancer, there wouldn't have been an NDE, and that would have meant no special vision to share with the world. Were any of those steps eliminated, the outcome could very well have been different. While I strongly believe that it's not necessary to reach the extreme state of an NDE in order to heal or have a great purpose in life, I can see that my personal path has led me to this point. Everything happens when we're ready for it to happen.

I'VE NOW WELL AND TRULY LEARNED THAT when I become centered—when I realize my place at the heart of the universe and *feel* my magnificence and my connection to all that is—time and distance become irrelevant. If you've ever been in a deep sleep and involved in an intricate dream that culminates in the ringing of a doorbell or phone, and you suddenly awaken to find your doorbell or phone *actually* ringing, then you've experienced timelessness. Even though the device only started going off a few seconds prior to your waking up, it feels as though the entire drama of your dream revolved around that final moment.

This is what life becomes like when you truly realize that *you're one with everything*. Time and space lose all significance. For example, I received the e-mail from Hay House at the exact moment that was appropriate for me, yet a whole drama was unfolding on Wayne Dyer's side that culminated in me receiving the message!

I want to say, too, that after my NDE, things got a whole lot easier. I no longer feared death, cancer, accidents or any of the myriad things that used to concern me . . . except for expanding out into the greater world! I've learned to trust the wisdom of my infinite self. I know that I—along with everyone else—am a powerful, magnificent, unconditionally loved, and loving force.

This energy flows through me, surrounds me, and is indistinguishable from me. It is, in fact, who and what I truly am; trusting in it is simply trusting myself. Allowing it to guide me, protect me, and give me all that's needed for my ultimate happiness and well-being happens simply by being myself. I need only be the magnificent love that I am and allow events and circumstances in my life to play out in the way that I *know* is always in my best long-term interest.

I detach myself from preconceived outcomes and trust that all is well. Being myself allows the wholeness of my unique magnificence to draw me in those directions most beneficial to me and to all others. This is really the only thing I have to do. And within that framework, everything that's truly mine comes into my life effortlessly, in the most magical and unexpected ways imaginable, demonstrating every day the power and love of who I truly am.

PART III

WHAT I'VE COME TO UNDERSTAND

CHAPTER 15

Why I Got Sick . . . and Healed

During my NDE, I experienced so much clarity that the question I get asked most frequently when sharing my story is: *So, what caused your cancer?* It's pretty understandable that most people are really interested in the answer!

But before I discuss this, I just want to put in a word of caution regarding the dangers inherent in this topic. One of the hazards is that what I say can come across sounding as though those who don't recover or those who still have cancer and other illnesses are in some way "less than" those who have healed. *This is just not true!*

It can also be frustrating if what I say sounds too simplistic, especially when you or someone you know is suffering. This is one of the first problems with language—sometimes words can cause more harm than good. I want to emphasize that anyone who still has cancer or who didn't heal is a completely magnificent person. The reasons for their illness lie in their personal journey and are probably related to their individual purpose. I can now see that my disease was part of why I'm here, and whether I chose to live or die, I wouldn't be any less magnificent.

I know there will be some who disagree with what I say about healing, which is perfectly fine. I'm only expressing what I felt happened within me at that time, in the hope that my words may help someone else.

As I said, the most frequent question people ask me is why I think I got cancer. I can sum up the answer in one word: *fear.*

What was I afraid of? Just about everything, including failing, being disliked, letting people down, and not being good enough. I also feared illness, cancer in particular, as well as the treatment for cancer. I was afraid of living, and I was terrified of dying.

Fear is very subtle, and it can creep up gradually without our even noticing it. Looking back, I see that most of us are taught from a very young age to be afraid, although I don't believe we're born this way.

One of the things I believe is that *we already are what we spend our lives trying to attain,* but we just don't realize it! We come into this life knowing our magnificence. I don't know why, but the world seems to erode it as we start to grow up.

This starts subtly at first, with little anxieties such as not being liked or not being good enough, perhaps because we look different from our peers—maybe we're of another race, too tall, too short, too fat, or too thin. We want so much to fit in. I don't recall ever being encouraged to be who I really was or to be true to myself, nor was I assured that it's okay to be different. All I remember is that little niggling voice of disapproval that I continually heard in the back of my head.

I was a people pleaser and feared disapproval, regardless of the source. I bent over backward to avoid people thinking ill of me; and over the years, I lost myself in the process. I was completely disconnected from who I was or what I wanted, because everything I did was designed to win approval—everyone's except my own. In fact, in the years leading up to my cancer, if anyone had asked me what I wanted in life, I would have had to say that I really didn't know. I was so wrapped up in cultural expectations, trying to be the person I was expected to be, that I really didn't know what was important to *me.*

After my best friend, Soni, and Danny's brother-in-law were both diagnosed with cancer, I started to develop a deep fear of the disease. I felt that if it could strike them, it could strike anyone, so I began to do everything I could to keep from getting sick. However, the more I read about prevention, the more I felt I had reason to be afraid. It seemed to me that everything caused cancer. I read about how pathogens in the environment and food were carcinogenic. Microwaves, using plastic containers for food, eating anything with preservatives, using mobile phones—they all seemed to cause cancer. The list just went on and on.

Not only was I afraid of the disease itself, I was also afraid of the treatment—chemotherapy. As I described, Soni died while on chemo, and this just exacerbated my fears.

Slowly, I found myself terrified of both dying and living. It was almost as if I were being caged by my fears. My experience of life was getting smaller and smaller, because to me, the world was a menacing place. And then I was diagnosed with cancer.

EVEN THOUGH I SEEMED TO BE FIGHTING MY DISEASE, I believed that cancer was a death sentence. I went through the motions of doing everything I could, but in the back of my mind, I still believed that I wasn't going to make it. And I was very, very scared of death.

The fact that researchers continually said they were "trying to find a cure for cancer" suggested to me that there was no known solution. This seemed to be an accepted fact, at least in the conventional medical world. Being told that conventional medicine was the only option, even though that discipline admitted it had no cure, was enough to send a deep feeling of dread right through to my core. The word *cancer* in itself was enough to cause fear, and knowing the scientific shortcomings just endorsed the feeling that I was going to die.

I still tried to do everything I possibly could, but the illness seemed to be progressing and getting worse. Although most people I knew advised me against it, I opted for alternative healing because I felt that with conventional therapy, I was doomed from the start. Instead, I took up every other modality I knew of, and as I mentioned earlier, I quit my job and devoted four years to this process.

I tried faith healing, praying, meditation, and energy-healing sessions. I read every book I could get my hands on about cancer, learning every possible connotation given to the disease. I worked on forgiveness therapy, and forgave everyone I knew—then forgave them again. I traveled through India and China, meeting Buddhist monks, Indian yogis, and enlightened masters, hoping that they'd help me find answers that would lead to healing. I tried being vegan, meditating on mountaintops, yoga, ayurveda, chakra balancing, Chinese herbal medicine, pranic healing, and Chi Gong.

But despite all this, my cancer just kept getting worse. My mind was in a total state of confusion as I continued to lose myself further and further in different healing modalities, trying everything just to stay alive while my health continued to deteriorate. As I described earlier, my body eventually stopped absorbing nutrients, and my muscles wasted away until I couldn't walk anymore. The wheelchair became my only form of mobility. My head hung from my neck like an oversized bowling ball, and I couldn't breathe without the portable oxygen tank that never left my side. When I slept, my husband stayed awake all night just to make sure I was still breathing. My mother helped look after me because I couldn't take care of myself. It was very difficult for all of us, and I could feel their pain in addition to my own.

I can't even begin to describe the intensity of the terror I was experiencing day after day, as my body continued to deteriorate. I was hanging onto life by my fingernails. I attended spiritual-healing groups and even was told that this was my choice. I also heard that the world is an illusion.

I became more frustrated and scared, wondering: *Why would I choose this? How do I choose differently? If this is an illusion, why does it feel so real? If God listens to all prayers, why isn't He listening to mine?* I'd been trying so hard to do all the forgiving, cleansing, healing, praying, and meditating that I could. I just couldn't understand why this was happening to me.

But when it finally became too difficult to hang on anymore, I let go. There was a total internal release. After cancer ravaging my body for more than four years, I was simply too weak to hold on . . . so I surrendered. I was tired. I knew the next step would be death, and I'd finally reached the point where I welcomed it. Anything had to be better than this.

That's when I went into the coma and my organs started to shut down. I knew nothing could be worse than what my family and I were going through. And so I began plunging toward death.

THE REALM I EXPERIENCED WHEN MY BODY shut down allowed me to see my own magnificence, undistorted by fear. I became aware of the greater power I had access to.

When I relinquished my hold on physical life, I didn't feel I needed to do anything in particular to enter the other realm, such as pray, chant, use mantras, forgiveness, or any other technique. Moving on was closer to doing absolutely *nothing*. It seemed more like saying to no one in particular: "Okay, I have nothing more to give. I surrender. Take me. Do what you will with me. Have your way."

While I was in that state of clarity in the other realm, I instinctively understood that I was dying because of all my fears. I wasn't expressing my true self because my worries were preventing me from doing so. I understood that the cancer wasn't a punishment or anything like that. It was just my own energy, manifesting as cancer because my fears weren't allowing me to express myself as the magnificent force I was meant to be.

In that expansive state, I realized how harshly I'd treated myself and judged myself throughout my life. There was nobody punishing me. I finally understood that it was *me* I hadn't forgiven, not other people. *I* was the one who was judging me, whom I'd forsaken, and whom I didn't love enough. It had nothing to do with anyone else. I saw myself as a beautiful child of the universe. Just the fact that I existed made me deserving of unconditional love. I realized that I didn't need to *do* anything to deserve this—not pray, nor beg, nor anything else. I saw that I'd never loved myself, valued myself, or seen the beauty of my own soul. Although the unconditional magnificence was always there for me, it felt as though physical life had somehow filtered it out or even eroded it away.

This understanding made me realize that I no longer had anything to fear. I saw what I—what all of us—have access to. And so I made one powerful choice: to come back. That decision, made from that awakened state, was the single most powerful driving force in my return. Once I woke up again in my body, I knew that every single cell would respond to the decision to come back, so I knew I was going to be fine.

Back in my physical self in the hospital, I understood that everything after that—all the tests, biopsies, and drugs—was being done to satisfy everyone around me. Although a lot of it was extremely painful, I knew that I'd be fine. My magnificent, infinite self had decided to continue to live and express through this body, so nothing in this world could affect the decision.

I WANT TO CLARIFY THAT MY HEALING wasn't so much born from a shift in my state of mind or beliefs as it was from finally allowing my true spirit to shine through. Many have asked me if something like positive thinking caused my recovery, and the answer is *no*. The state I was in during my NDE was way beyond the mind, and I healed because my damaging thoughts were simply out of the way completely. I was not in a state of thinking, but a state of *being*. It was pure consciousness—what I call magnificence! This state of Oneness transcends duality. I was able to get in touch with who I truly am, the part of me that's eternal, infinite, and encompasses the Whole. This definitely wasn't a case of mind over matter.

I don't advocate that if we "believe" a certain way, we'll eliminate disease or create an ideal life. That can sometimes be too simplistic. Instead, I'm more focused on self-awareness, which is different. Becoming entrenched in beliefs that no longer serve us can keep us locked in a state of duality and put us in a constant state of judgment. What we endorse is considered "good" or "positive," and what we don't believe in is not.

This also puts us in the position of needing to defend our beliefs when others don't agree. And when we invest too much of our energy in defense, we become reluctant to let go, even when ideas no longer serve us. That's when our beliefs start to own us instead of the other way around.

Having awareness, on the other hand, just means realizing what exists and what's possible—without judgment. Awareness doesn't need defending. It expands with growth and can be all-encompassing, bringing us closer to the state of Oneness. This is where miracles take place. In contrast, beliefs only allow what we deem credible while keeping out everything else.

So no, it wasn't my beliefs that caused me to heal. My NDE was a state of pure awareness, which is a state of complete suspension of all previously held doctrine and dogma. This allowed my body to "reset" itself. In other words, an absence of belief was required for my healing.

In the moment that I completely let go of my strong desire to stay alive, I experienced death. And in dying, I realized that it wasn't my time. When I was willing to let go of what I wanted, I received what was truly mine. I've realized that the latter is always the greater gift.

Since my NDE, I've learned that strongly held ideologies actually work against me. Needing to operate out of concrete beliefs limits my experiences because it keeps me within the realm of only what I know—and my knowledge is limited. And if I restrict myself to only what I'm able to conceive, I'm holding back my potential and what I allow into my life. However, if I can accept that my understanding is incomplete, and if I'm able to be comfortable with uncertainty, this opens me up to the realm of infinite possibilities.

I've found that subsequent to my NDE, I'm at my strongest when I'm able to let go, when I suspend my beliefs as well as disbeliefs, and leave myself open to *all* possibilities. That also seems to be when I'm able to experience the most internal clarity and synchronicities. My sense is that the very act of *needing* certainty is a hindrance to experiencing greater levels of awareness. In contrast, the process of letting go and releasing all attachment to any belief or outcome is cathartic and healing. The dichotomy is that for true healing to occur, I must let go of the need to be healed and just enjoy and trust in the ride that is life.

It was important for me to become aware that I'm far more than my biology, that I'm something infinitely greater. And again, I'd like to reiterate that illnesses are not our fault! Thinking that they are can be frustrating to anyone who's sick. But I *am* saying that our biology responds to our awareness; our children, animals, and surroundings do, too. Our consciousness can change the conditions of the planet in a much larger way than we realize. This is because we're all connected—I can't say this often enough!

To me, the first step to conscious awareness is understanding how nature intended things to be. It means being aware of our bodies and our surroundings and being able to respect the essence of things without needing them to be different—and this includes ourselves. We must understand the magnificence of how the universe *intended* us to be without needing to change. I don't have to try to live up to other people's expectations of perfection and then feel inadequate when I fail miserably.

I'm at my most powerful when I allow myself to be who life intended me to be—which is why my healing occurred only when all conscious action on my part had completely ceased and the life force took over. In other words, I'm at my most powerful when I am working *with* life rather than *against* it.

It's all very well for me to talk about healing after I've experienced it, or for me to tell you to just trust and let go, letting the flow of life take over; but when you're going through a really low period, it's difficult to do—or even to know where to begin. However, I think the answer is simpler than it seems, and it's one of the best-kept secrets of our time: the importance of *self-love.* You may frown or cringe at the thought, but I can't stress enough how important it is to cultivate a deep love affair with yourself.

I don't recall *ever* being encouraged to cherish myself—in fact, it would never even have occurred to me to do so. It's commonly thought of as being selfish. But my NDE allowed me to realize that this was the key to my healing.

In the tapestry of life, we're all connected. Each one of us is a gift to those around us, helping each other be who we are, weaving a perfect picture together. When I was in the NDE state, it all became so clear to me because I understood that to *be me* is to *be love*. This is the lesson that saved my life.

Many of us still believe that we have to work at being loving, but that means living in duality, because there's a giver and a receiver. Realizing that we *are* love transcends this. It means understanding that there's no separation between you and me, and if I'm aware that I am love, then I know that you are, too. If I care for myself, then I automatically feel the same for you!

In my NDE state, I realized that the entire universe is composed of unconditional love, and I'm an expression of this. Every atom, molecule, quark, and tetraquark, is made of love. I can be nothing else, because this is my essence and the nature of the entire universe. Even things that seem negative are all part of the infinite, unconditional spectrum of love. In fact, Universal life-force energy *is* love, and I'm composed of Universal energy! Realizing this made me understand that I didn't have to try to become someone else in order to be worthy. I already am all that I could attempt to be.

Similarly, when we know that we *are* love, we don't need to work at *being* loving toward others. Instead, we just have to be true to ourselves, and we become instruments of loving energy, which touches everyone we come into contact with.

Being love also means being aware of the importance of nurturing my own soul, taking care of my own needs, and not putting myself last all the time. This allows me to be true to myself at all times and to treat myself with total respect and kindness. It also lets me view what may be interpreted as imperfections and mistakes with no judgment, seeing only opportunities to experience and to learn with unconditional love.

PEOPLE ASK ME WHETHER THERE'S SUCH A THING as too much self-love. Where's the line, they ask, where it starts to become selfish or egotistical? To me, there's no such possibility. There is no line.

Selfishness comes from *lack* of self-love. Our planet is suffering from this, as we humans are, along with too much insecurity, judgment, and conditioning. In order to truly care for someone unconditionally, I have to feel that way toward myself. I can't give away what I don't have. To say that I hold another in higher regard than myself isn't real and means I'm only performing.

When I'm *being love,* I don't get drained, and I don't need people to behave a certain way in order to feel cared for or to share my magnificence with them. They're automatically getting my love as a result of me being my true self. And when I am nonjudgmental of myself, I feel that way toward others.

In light of this, I've learned that it's important not to be too hard on myself if I'm experiencing challenges. Oftentimes, the problem isn't the cause of the apparent conflict. Instead, it's the judgment I have for myself. When I stop being my own worst enemy and start loving myself more, I automatically have less and less friction with the world around me. I become more tolerant and accepting.

When we're each aware of our own magnificence, we don't feel the need to control others, and we won't allow ourselves to be controlled. When I awoke into my infinite self, I was amazed to understand that my life could be dramatically different just by realizing that I *am* love, and I always have been. I don't have to do anything to deserve it. Understanding this means that I'm working with life-force energy, whereas *performing* at being loving is working against it.

Realizing that I *am* love was the most important lesson I learned, allowing me to release all fear, and that's the key that saved my life.

CHAPTER 16

Infinite Selves and Universal Energy

During my near-death experience, it felt as if I were connected to the entire universe and everything contained within it; and it seemed that the cosmos was alive, dynamic, and conscious. I found that every thought, emotion, or action I made while expressing through the physical body had an effect on the Whole. In fact, in that realm of Oneness, it felt as though the whole universe were an extension of *me*. This realization has, of course, dramatically changed the way I view things. We're all co-creating this world and our lives within it through our emotions, thoughts, and actions.

Language isn't an adequate tool for expressing something that can't be perceived with our five physical senses, so it's challenging to find the right words to express my understanding of what took place during the experience. However, I'll do my best in this chapter to share as clearly as possible what I sense about this world, how we move through it, and how it's changing for the better.

First, it's important to understand that my NDE wasn't like any other event I've experienced. It didn't have a clear beginning and end. It was more like a door that once opened, never closes. It initiated ongoing, progressive, deeper understanding and new possibilities that never end.

Because words are a poor tool to express this kind of phenomena, what I write here is only meant to stir the appropriate emotions within you. Even after I share this, my own understanding will continue to grow and expand. Words taken literally or held as ultimate truth can keep us stagnant and stuck, holding on to old ideologies. I now know that everything I need is already contained within me and is completely accessible if I allow myself to open up to what I sense is true for me . . . and the same is true for you.

BEFORE MY NDE, PROBABLY BECAUSE OF MY CULTURE, I used to think that the purpose of life was to attain nirvana—that is, to evolve beyond the reincarnation cycle of birth and death, striving never to come back into the physical. If I'd grown up completely immersed in Western culture, maybe I would have been trying to get to heaven. This is actually a fairly common goal, regardless of culture—to live in such a way as to secure a perfect afterlife.

But after my NDE, I feel differently. Even though I know I'll go on living beyond this plane, and I don't fear physical death anymore, I've lost my desire to be anywhere but the place I am now. Interestingly, I've become more grounded and focused on seeing the perfection of life in this moment, rather than focusing on the other realm.

This is primarily because the concept of reincarnation in its conventional form of a progression of lifetimes, running sequentially one after the other, wasn't supported by my NDE. I realized that time doesn't move in a linear fashion unless we're using the filter of our physical bodies and minds. Once we're no longer limited by our earthly senses, every moment exists simultaneously. I've come to think that the concept of reincarnation is really just an interpretation, a way for our intellect to make sense of all existence happening at once.

We think in terms of "time passing," but in my NDE, it felt as though time just *is*, and we're moving through it. This means that not only do all points of time exist simultaneously, but also that in the other realm, we can go faster, slower, or even backward and sideways.

In the physical plane, however, our sensory organs limit us. Our eyes take in what they see in this instant; our ears hear in the same way. The mind can only exist in one moment, and then it strings those moments together to form a linear progression. But when we spill out of our bodies, we cross all time and space with awareness—not sight, hearing, touch, taste, or smell. We're pure consciousness.

I experienced this while in the NDE state. I was aware of my brother on a plane coming to see me and of conversations the doctors were having outside my room and down the hall. I understood many aspects of my future life, as they would be panning out, as well as what would happen if I didn't come back and live. This showed me that time, space, and solid matter don't always exist as we normally think of them. During my NDE, I felt that I could focus on any point in time that I needed to access.

Because of this, I believe that when someone has a glimpse of what have previously been interpreted as "past lives," they're actually accessing *parallel* or *simultaneous* existences, because all time exists at once. And because we're all connected, it's possible to achieve states of consciousness where glimpses of others' reality seep through into our present moment, entering our consciousness as though they were memories.

My new perspective has made me wonder about our focus and purpose, if reincarnation and time itself don't exist the way that so many of us were raised to believe. What if all our goals are the wrong way around? What if heaven or nirvana is actually *here* in physical expression, and not *there* in the afterlife?

I SENSE THAT WE CHOOSE TO INCARNATE into a physical body in order to express love, passion, and the full range of other human emotions not available to us separately in the state of pure awareness and Oneness. What if this life on this planet is the main show, where the action is, and where we wanted to be?

This reality is a playground of expression. It looks as though we aren't here to learn or gather experiences for the afterlife. There doesn't seem to be much purpose in that because we don't need any of it there. Rather, we're here to experience and evolve this physical universe and our own lives within it. I made my decision to return when I realized that life here was the most desirable state for me at this time. We don't have to wait until we die to experience nirvana. *Our true magnificence exists right now!*

The reason why humans are so vulnerable and fearful around this subject is because we create our ideas of the afterlife and our gods in human terms. We assign to these concepts the same physical properties and fallible values that we posses and are vulnerable to—values such as fear, retribution, judgment, and punishment. And then we project all our strength and power onto our own creations.

But if all time and experience exist right now, and we're simply moving through it as we express our magnificence in a physical world, then we have nothing to fear. We don't have to live in anxiety about what comes next. We can recognize the energy that we're already a part of, and we can *be love* in every aspect of our lives.

It's unfortunate that we keep searching outside ourselves for answers—in religion, medicine, scientific study, books, and other people. We think the truth is somewhere out there, still elusive. Yet by doing this, we're only getting more and more lost, appearing to move away from who we truly are. The entire universe is within us. My answers are inside of me, and yours lie within you, too. Everything that seemingly happens externally is occurring in order to trigger something within us, to expand us and take us back to who we truly are.

I often use the phrase *infinite self* in place of terms such as *higher self, soul,* and *spirit.* In order to be a little clearer, understand that I'm referring to the part of me that was aware during the NDE that I'm not just my body—the part of me that felt I was one with every single thing. I was merging with pure consciousness as an infinite, magnificent being, feeling the clarity of why I'm in this body and life at this point in time. This is also the part of me that understood that the illusion of separation is created by identifying too strongly with the external.

I believe that when we leave our physical bodies, our infinite selves are all connected. In the pure consciousness state, we're all One. Many people have felt this unity during intense spiritual experiences or out in nature. When we work with animals or have pets, we feel it, too. We sometimes experience synchronicity and even extrasensory perception (ESP) and other such phenomena as a result of our being One with all creation, but because most people aren't aware of it, it doesn't happen as often as it could.

In truth, I'm not my body, my race, religion, or other beliefs, and neither is anyone else. The real self is infinite and much more powerful—a complete and whole entity that isn't broken or damaged in any way. The infinite me already contains all the resources I need to navigate through life, because I'm One with Universal energy. In fact, I *am* Universal energy.

DURING MY NDE, THERE WAS NOTHING outside of my greater awareness because I was one with the entirety of Universal energy. It felt as though I encompassed totality. In that state, there was total clarity and all became known. I seemed to become everything, and I existed in everything.

The ability to see my own magnificence and to realize that the universe and I are one and the same caused my healing. I became conscious that there isn't an external creation separate from me—because the word *external* suggests separation and duality. Living with this awareness allows me to continue to interact in the physical world with strength, love, and courage.

To explain this from another perspective, although I've been using the words *Universal energy,* know that I can just as easily say *chi, prana,* or *ki.* These words mean "life-force energy" in Mandarin, Hindi, and Japanese respectively. This is the *chi* in Tai Chi and Chi Gong, and it's the *ki* in Reiki. In a nutshell, it's the Source of life, and it runs through every living thing. In fact, it fills the entire universe and is inseparable from it.

Chi has no judgment and doesn't discriminate. It flows through us whether we're an elevated guru or a sea slug. It's useful to think about this, because once we describe the energy with a different word—such as *Source, God, Krishna, Buddha,* or whatever —it can be difficult for some of us to see beyond the name. These terms mean different things to different people, and also seem to impose form upon the infinite. There are often certain expectations attached to these labels, and many of them keep us locked in duality so that we view this energy as an entity separate from us. But Universal energy, like our pure state of consciousness, needs to remain limitless and formless so that it can become one with us and create healing, magic, and miracles.

I felt strongly during my NDE that we're all connected to this Universal energy; we're all One with it. Each of us has this magnificent, magical life force coursing through every single cell. It's not some external entity, but rather a state of being—an internal phenomenon. It's inside, outside, and all around. It doesn't matter what race, religion, culture, or belief system we belong to. We're connected to it just because we're alive—in fact, we *are* this universal current. We don't have to do anything, be anything, or prove anything to access it. We're all magnificent, powerful beings, and we all have access to it because it and we are one and the same.

The only thing that can keep me from being aware of this energy is my mind—that is, my thoughts, particularly my self-limiting beliefs about myself. The deep release I mentioned earlier that took me to the NDE was actually my intellect completely letting go, taking my self-limiting beliefs with it and allowing universal energy to take over. Once my mind got out of the way, the floodgates opened. Instead of fighting against the nature of the universe in order to heal, I allowed chi to flow on its own terms.

It can be tricky at first to distinguish what's motivating us. The difference is that the mind is more about *doing,* and the soul is more about *being.* The infinite self is our essence. It's who we truly are, as I described in the last chapter when I explained the importance of being love. The intellect is just a tool for navigating through this life. It figures out how to make enough money to put food on the table and make the rent, while the soul only wants to express itself.

The infinite self is where we have our instincts and intuition. If we're buying a house, the mind will narrow down the options by choosing a practical location, setting a budget, and so on. The final decision on a specific place to live, however, may be made purely by gut feeling. We just get a good sense about a certain place, and there's no logical reason that we can explain. That's the infinite self.

Sometimes our complicated lives make us forget that we're connected to Universal energy and that we have these natural abilities. We stop listening to ourselves and start to give our power away to external forces such as bosses, teachers, and friends. Blocking our feelings also breaks down our awareness of our own magnificence because emotions are a doorway into the soul. But we're complex beings, and we try to control how we feel.

When we live completely from the mind over a period of time, we lose touch with the infinite self, and then we begin to feel lost. This happens when we're in *doing* mode all the time, rather than *being.* The latter means living from the soul and is a state of allowing. It means letting ourselves be who and what we are without judgment. *Being* doesn't mean that we don't do anything. It's just that our actions stem from following our emotions and feelings while staying present in the moment. *Doing,* on the other hand, is future focused, with the mind creating a series of tasks that take us from here to there in order to achieve a particular outcome, regardless of our current emotional state.

I have discovered that to determine whether my actions stem from "doing" or "being," I only need to look at the emotion behind my everyday decisions. Is it fear, or is it passion? If everything I do each day is driven by passion and a zest for living, then I'm "being," but if my actions are a result of fear, then I'm in "doing" mode.

When we feel off track, we think there's something wrong with us—something we have to do or get in order to right ourselves—so we go searching outside for answers. We look to others in the hope that they'll fix us. We may feel better for a little while, but it's usually short-lived, and we eventually end up feeling worse. However, when we really start to tune in to who life intended us to be—and we're attuned to the emotions that motivate us— we connect with the soul of our magnificence. We feel clarity when we allow this connection and take our power back, and our lives start to work.

When we come from this place of *being* who we are, we can choose to learn from external gurus, teachers, books, or spiritual philosophies. We become aware of our own inner magnificence and truth, instead of believing that others have power that we don't. In fact, when we realize our magnificence and live in our true nature of love, we'll synchronistically attract the right teacher, book, or spiritual philosophy at the right time!

UNFORTUNATELY, BEING UNAWARE OF OUR OWN magnificence can have effects that seem far greater than simply feeling lost, although it's all of the same essence. During my NDE, it felt to me that all judgment, hatred, jealousy, and fear stem from people not realizing their true greatness. Lacking awareness of our perfection keeps us feeling small and insignificant, and this goes *against* the natural flow of life-force energy—that which we really are. We go against ourselves.

The way I see it, if we were encouraged to express who we truly are, we'd all be very loving beings, each bringing our uniqueness to the world. Problems and strife come as a result of our *not knowing* who we are and not being able to show our inner beauty. We've created so much judgment about what's "perfect," which leads to doubt and competitiveness. Since we feel as though we're not good enough, we go around acting out. However, if each of us became aware of our magnificence and felt good about ourselves, it seems to me the only thing we'd have to share is our unique nature, expressed outwardly in a loving manner that reflects our self-care.

It follows that the problems we see in the world aren't from the judgment or hatred we have for *others* but for *ourselves*. Just as the key to my healing was unconditional self-love that eliminated fear, the key to a better world is for everyone to care for themselves the same way, realizing their true worth. If we stopped judging ourselves, we'd automatically find less and less need to condemn others. We'd begin to notice their true perfection. The universe is contained within us, and what we experience externally is only a reflection.

I believe that at the core, no one is truly bad—that evil is only a product of our fears, the same way my cancer was. From the magnificent perspective, even criminals are victims of their own limitations, fear, and pain. If they'd had true self-awareness to begin with, they never would have caused any harm. A different mind-set—for example, a complete state of trust instead of fright—can turn around even the most depraved person, the same way that I reversed the extreme disease of my cancer.

Because most people don't live in that clarity of self-awareness, laws, judgment, rewards, and punishments are required to keep folks from harming each other. If everyone were aware of their own magnificence, then we'd no longer be driven by fear. We wouldn't need rules and jails . . . or hospitals.

IF EVERY SINGLE PERSON SUDDENLY BECAME aware of their true perfection and magnificence—let's say that everyone on the planet had a spiritually transformative experience—our manifest world would change to reflect that new state. People would be more self-empowered and far less fearful and competitive, which would lead to more tolerance for each other. Crime rates would drop dramatically. Our immune systems would be stronger from less stress and fear, so there would be fewer illnesses. Priorities would change because we'd no longer be driven by greed, which is another facet of fear. Children would grow up *being love*—being stronger, healthier, and more trusting. They'd live on a planet that naturally supports this way of life rather than in a place that's hostile to it.

Despite this vision, I don't feel the need to change anyone else, let alone the world. Going out and altering things suggests I judge them to be wrong, therefore I need to fix them to match my own vision or ideology. Instead, everything is as it should be at this point in time. I know my only work is to *be*. My job here is to be myself—an expression of the love that I am—and to see the perfection in myself, others, and the world around me as I continue to live in the physical plane. That's all that any of us needs to be.

I understand the roles that everyone in my family and my larger circle play in my life and I in theirs. If I'm not true to myself, then others around me aren't able to be themselves either. Only by being my unique self can I allow others to interact with me on the level of their own infinite selves.

As long as I have this awareness, I feel at one with Universal energy as it flows through my life, unfolding in miraculous and synchronistic ways. I become energized instead of drained—lifted up by *being* instead of brought down by *doing*, working *with* universal energy rather than *against* it. As I continue in this manner, my life takes on a Zen-like quality, in that I'm present to the point that everything has an almost surreal, guided feeling. It's not always easy, but it's certainly made life more fun! I'm definitely still a work in progress, but this is pretty much all I have to do—just be the love I am, be *who* I am. My external universe will fall into place as a result of that, and the same is true on a grand scale.

Just as we each create our own lives moment by moment with our thoughts and emotions, we've also collectively decided what's humanly possible and what isn't. Similarly, we also think our morals and values are absolute, but actually they're just a bunch of thoughts and beliefs that we've adopted over time as being true. They're a construct of our minds and a product of our cultures, just like all the gender expectations that shaped my thinking during my early years. Because I believed these values to be absolutely true, they affected who I was. As a whole, the reality we've created reflects this unawareness. If everyone's thoughts and beliefs were different, then we'd have created a different planet.

It seems to me that this world is always a culmination of all our collective thoughts and beliefs where they currently stand. We only expand at the rate we're capable of handling at any given point, individually or collectively. We still judge perpetrators of crime as exactly that—criminals who deserve to be condemned, not only in this life but in the afterlife as well! We're still unable to see them as victims of fear, creations of a reality that we, as a whole, have built.

When each of us is able to look into the eyes of even our worst enemies and see our own eyes looking back, then we'll see true transformation of the human race. One by one, each one of us can focus on creating reality for ourselves based on our own truths, rather than blindly following what has been set up by our collective beliefs and thoughts. By expanding our awareness on an individual level, we'll be effecting change on a universal level.

Each one of us is like a single thread in a huge tapestry, woven in a complex and colorful pattern. We may be only one strand, yet we're all integral to the finished image. We affect the lives of others just by choosing whether or not to be our true selves. Our only obligation to others, our only purpose, is to express our uniqueness and allow others to do the same.

Realizing that the Light, the magnificent Universal energy is within us and *is us*, changes us as individuals because we're open and ready. In this way, a slower, deeper shift can take place in the world. In the next chapter, I'll explore even more of what I've come to understand about living in this plane.

CHAPTER 17

Allowing and Being Yourself

I know I've said it before, but it bears repeating: I now live my life from joy instead of from fear. This is the one very simple difference between who I was before my NDE and who I am today.

Before, without even realizing it, everything I did was to avoid pain or to please other people. I was caught up in doing, pursuing, searching, and achieving; and I was the last person I ever took into consideration. My life was driven by fear—of displeasing others, of failing, of being selfish, and of not being good enough. In my own head, I always fell short.

Since my NDE, I don't feel that I came back to *accomplish* anything. I only came back to *be*. Because of this, everything I do comes from love. I don't worry anymore about trying to get things right or complying with rules or doctrines. I just follow my heart and know that I can't go wrong when I do so. Ironically, I end up pleasing more people than my old self ever did, just because I'm so much happier and more liberated!

This has a big impact on my health as well. Since I now see myself as an infinite being, the physical takes care of itself because it's only a reflection of what's going on within my soul. Unconditional self-love increases my energy tremendously, and the universe acts in kind.

The external world mirrors what we feel about ourselves. By letting go of any negative self-judgment, we allow our world to transform; and as it does so, we'll be able to feel greater and greater trust. The more we're able to trust, the more we're able to let go of trying to control the outcome. When we try to move with this flow rather than adhere dogmatically to the doctrines of others or the beliefs we once had that no longer serve us, we more accurately reflect who and what we truly are.

As I'VE DESCRIBED, UNTIL MY NDE, I'd always been searching outward for guidance, whether it was seeking approval from my peers or bosses or simply looking to others for answers. I followed the opinions, advice, teachings, and laws that were laid down by other people, whether they felt good for me or not. Often, I adhered to the rituals and teachings out of fear, just in case they were right and had information that I didn't.

During my NDE, I discovered that in listening to all these external voices, I'd lost myself. Doing things "just in case" means doing them out of fear. So these days, I don't follow any established methodology, order, ritual, dogma, or doctrine. In fact, one of my biggest rules is that there should never be any hard and fast rules! I just pay attention to whatever *feels* right at the time. For me, life is a spiritual experience, and I'm changing and evolving all the time.

If we're energetic beings inseparable from the Universal life force, we don't need any outside system to make decisions for us or tell us how our energy can be raised or lowered. We're all unique, so no one can really make blanket rules about what's right for us. However, this is what many organized spiritual systems and religions seem to do. Once a structure is established, everyone is expected to follow the same tenets. Those who choose not to are judged negatively, and that's how and why organized religions create divisiveness and strife instead of the unity that they're trying to establish with those very rules. Following a religious path doesn't necessarily exempt us from living a life of fear or even victimizing others. Following a *personal* spiritual path, however, means to follow the promptings of our own inner being and taps into the infinite self we all are at our core.

It's clear how fallible organized systems are once we cross cultures. Indian and Chinese spiritual and healing systems completely contradict each other. Hindus believe eating animal flesh is a sin, while the Chinese believe it's unhealthy *not* to eat meat. Similarly, Indians have a system called *vastu* that has the same purpose as *feng shui* but is in direct conflict with the Chinese rules. I used to get so lost with each authority endorsing something that conflicts with all the others. Not knowing which one to use can actually create a lot of fear—or at least anxiety about getting it wrong.

So in the end, my NDE brought me back to myself. I believe this is the most powerful idea for each of us: realizing that we're here to discover and honor *our own individual path.* It doesn't matter whether we renounce the material world and meditate on a mountaintop for 20 years or create a billion-dollar multinational company that employs thousands of people, giving them each a livelihood. We can attend a temple or church, sit on the beach, drink a margarita, take in a glorious sunset with a loved one, or walk through the park enjoying an ice cream. Ultimately, whichever path we choose is the right one for us, and none of these options are any more or less spiritual than the others.

I'm not saying that I'm against organized religion, but I *am* skeptical of any message when it leads to all the divisiveness, strife, and killing that go on in this world in the name of religion, when in truth, we're all One—all facets of the same Whole. Human beings are so varied that some fare better with organized religion or spiritual paths, whereas others don't. If we simply live in a way that nurtures us and allows us to express our creativity, letting us see our own magnificence, that's the best we can possibly do. To advocate any option or doctrine as being the one true way would only serve to limit who we are and what we've come here to be.

WE DON'T HAVE TO ACTUALLY "WORK" AT doing anything—like following specific rituals or dogma—to stay in touch with our magnificence. We can if we want to, if it brings us pleasure to do so, but it's not a requirement. Simply by following our internal guidance, we find what's right for us, including the methodology we use to look for it. We know we're on the right track when we feel ourselves at the center of our love without judgment of ourselves or others, and we recognize our true magnificence within the infinite Whole.

For example, prayer can bring great comfort to some people in times of need, and also for self-discovery. It may have a positive effect on well-being because of the process of letting go and handing over all burdens. As a result, people who pray may feel lighter and more uplifted, which contributes not only to their own well-being, but also to others since we're all connected. Any positivity you bring to yourself, you're bringing to the Whole.

However, I don't believe that those who pray are any more or less connected than those who don't. We all have our own way of recognizing that infinite space within us, and for some it may be prayer. For others, it can be music, art, being in nature, or even pursuing knowledge and technology—whatever brings out our passion, creativity and purpose for living. In other words, it's not prayer in and of itself that makes some of us more aware of our magnificence than others. Rather, it's choosing to conduct our lives by connecting with our own internal passion, bringing out a Zen-like quality and giving our lives meaning and a feeling of unity.

I personally don't feel the need to pray to an external god who's separate from me, because I know that I'm always One with the Universe, 100 percent of the time. Thus, I feel that my life is a prayer in itself. I do find meditation very helpful because it quiets my mind and helps me bring focus to that central point of awareness where I feel my connection with everything contained within the Whole. Meditation might not create this uplifting feeling for others, and that's fine. It's important to do what resonates on a personal level.

If you feel you can follow a system effortlessly, or if it's fun, that's great! But the minute it starts to be hard work or feel like a means of controlling your emotions or thoughts, it probably won't work very well for you. The state of *pure allowing* seems like the place where most positive change can occur. Let yourself be you, no matter who you are, embracing anything that makes you feel alive.

ALTHOUGH I STRONGLY BELIEVE THAT the best thing I can do for myself *and* others is to consciously keep myself uplifted and do what makes me feel happy, you may be surprised to learn that I don't advocate "positive thinking" as a blanket prescription. It's true that since all of life is connected, keeping myself in high spirits has a larger impact, as it is also what I'm putting out to the Whole.

However, if and when I notice negative thoughts creeping in, it seems best to allow them to pass through with acceptance and without judgment. When I try to suppress or force myself to change my feelings, the more I push them away, the more they push back. I just allow it all to flow through me, without judgment, and I find that the thoughts and emotions will pass. As a result, the right path for me unfolds in a totally natural way, letting me be who I truly am.

Sweeping statements such as "Negative thoughts attracts negativity in life" aren't necessarily true, and can make people who are going through a challenging time feel even worse. It can also create fear that they're going to attract even more negativity with their thoughts. Using this idea indiscriminately often makes people going through seemingly tough times feel as though *they're* bad for attracting such events, and that's just not true. If we start to believe that it's our negative thoughts that are creating any unpleasant situations, we can become paranoid about what we're thinking. On the contrary, it actually has less to do with our thoughts than with our emotions, especially what we feel about *ourselves*.

It's also not the case that attracting positive things is simply about keeping upbeat. I can't say this strongly enough, but *our feelings about ourselves* are actually the most important barometer for determining the condition of our lives! In other words, being true to ourselves is more important than just trying to stay positive!

I allow myself to feel negatively about things that upset me because it's much better to experience real emotions than to bottle them up. Once again, it's about *allowing* what I'm actually feeling, rather than fighting against it. The very act of permitting without judgment is an act of self-love. This act of kindness toward myself goes much further in creating a joyful life than falsely pretending to feel optimistic.

Sometimes when we see someone who's really upbeat, effervescent, and kind, but whose life is crumbling, we may think, *See? This "being positive" thing doesn't work.* But here's the issue: we don't know that individual's inner dialogue. We don't know what other people are telling themselves day in and day out, or whether they're emotionally happy. And most important, we don't know whether they love and value themselves!

Because of what I realized in my NDE, I feel it's so important not to have judgment and fear toward myself. When my inner dialogue is telling me that I'm safe, unconditionally loved, and accepted, I then radiate this energy outward and change my external world accordingly. My outer life is actually only a reflection of my inner state.

It's not important whether I'm having a bad day or a bad week. It's more important how I'm *feeling about myself* while I'm facing this day or week. It's about trusting the process even as I face a difficult time and not being afraid to feel anxiety, sadness, or fear, rather than suppressing everything until those emotions pass. It's about allowing myself to be true to who I am. Because of this, the feelings will dissipate and occur less and less frequently.

Before my NDE, I used to suppress my upsetting emotions a lot, because I used to believe that they would attract negativity in my life. In addition, I didn't want to concern others, so I tried to control my thoughts and force myself to be positive. But I now understand that the key is to always honor who you truly are and allow yourself to be in your own truth.

Every segment of time is totally unique, and as each moment has passed, it can't be replicated in this physical plane. I've learned to be comfortable with that and to live in the moment. As much as possible, I try not to carry any emotional baggage from one instant to the next. Instead I try to see each moment as a clean slate, bringing with it new possibilities. So I do what uplifts me or brings me the most pleasure and joy at that time—and while that might mean meditating, it could just as well mean that I go shopping or eat chocolates, if that's what I feel like.

Living more in harmony with who we truly are isn't just forcing ourselves to repeat positive thoughts. It really means being and doing things that make us happy, things that arouse our passion and bring out the best in us, things that make us feel good—and it also means loving ourselves unconditionally. When we're flowing in this way and feeling upbeat and energized about life, we're in touch with our magnificence. When we can find that within us, things really start to get exciting, and we find synchronicities happening all around us.

SYNCHRONICITY AND THE IDEA OF ATTRACTION have been given a lot of attention in recent years. The thought of things falling into place effortlessly because we're attracting them is alluring, but I prefer to think in terms of *allowing*, rather than *attracting*.

As I've said, we're one with the universe, our purpose is to be our magnificent selves, and the external world is only a reflection of what's inside us. The breakdown in my life came from my focus outward, the comparisons I made, and the competition this creates. I used to have the feeling that there wasn't enough for everyone, which causes greed and competitiveness. I needed to convince others to believe and think the way I did, instead of embracing our uniqueness and differences.

All these feelings came from a view that the universe is lacking and limited, when it's actually infinite. It's capable of growing and encompassing as much as we are. It's up to us to expand and allow in as much as we want, but it has to be done from the inside out, not the other way around.

Once I realized that there's nothing outside my infinite self, I could begin to focus on viewing myself as an ongoing work of perfection—but in a way that's dynamic, not static. Like a kaleidoscope that turns from one exquisite image to the next, perfection is constantly in motion. To me, this means seeing beauty in the journey and in the apparent mistakes as they take me to another level of understanding. My aim is to feel good enough about myself to get to a point of trust, and in that state, to let go of the outcome. When I began observing my own flawlessness, I started to notice my external world reflecting this. I was attracting what's best for me, which is also the best thing I can do for the universe.

Going out and changing the world doesn't work for me, as I've said before. It only feeds into the same judgmental energy that's causing problems in the first place since it stems from the opinion that something is wrong and needs to be changed. Instead, letting go of attachment to any way of believing or thinking has made me feel more expanded and almost transparent so that universal energy can just flow through me. More positive coincidences happen in my life when I'm in this state of allowing.

We always attract the perfect results, and like calls to like. So the kinder I am to myself, the more outward events will reflect that. The harder and more judgmental I am toward myself, the more my situation will match it. The universe always proves me right in my opinion of myself!

Previously, I used to *pursue,* feeling as though I had to do, get, and achieve. However, the very act of going after something stems from fear—we're afraid of not having what we truly want. It keeps us stuck in duality, because the focus is on the inherent separation between the hunter and the quarry. Now, however, I no longer chase anything. Instead, I *allow.*

For example, when I feel an incredible desire for where I want my life to go, I know that if I were to pursue it aggressively, this would only cause me to fight against universal energy. The more effort I have to put into trying to attain it, the more I know that I am doing something wrong. Allowing, on the other hand, doesn't require effort. It feels more like a release, because it means realizing that since everything is One, that which I intend to get is already mine.

The process of allowing happens by first trusting, and then by always being true to who I am. In this way, I will only attract that which is truly mine, and it all happens at the rate I'm comfortable with. I can keep focusing on what worries me or what I think I need or find lacking, and my life won't move toward what I'd like to experience. It will just stay the way it is now, because I'm paying attention to my fears and what upsets me or leaves me feeling unfulfilled, instead of expanding my awareness by trusting and allowing new experiences. So I can let the picture materialize slower or faster, depending on how quickly I want to let go of my worries and relax into the process. The more attached I am to certain ways of thinking or outcomes or the more fearful I am of new adventures, the slower the development will be, because I'm not open to the process. I'm not allowing universal energy to flow through me naturally.

Having said all that, I don't actually sit and ponder every choice or possibility. All I really do within each moment is to consciously *live* in that space, which is done internally, not externally. Outside, there's nothing to pursue and nothing to attract. And since the universe is within, whatever I experience inside myself affects the Whole.

Since the tapestry of all time has already been woven, everything I could ever want to happen in my life already exists in that infinite, nonphysical plane. My only task is to expand my earthly self enough to let it into this realm. So if there's something I desire, the idea isn't to go out and get it, but to expand my own consciousness to allow universal energy to bring it into my reality here.

Pursuing what I desire only reinforces separation, whereas *allowing* means realizing that since we're all One and everything is connected, that which I desire is already mine.

CHAPTER 18

Questions and Answers

In the months and years following my NDE, I've had many opportunities to speak to various groups throughout the world about my experience. The following are some of the questions and answers that have resulted from these conversations.

Q: How do you define the "unconditional love" that you experienced in the other realm, and how does it differ from the love we experience in this physical reality?

A: The love in the other realm is very different in that it's pure in essence. It has no agenda and no expectations, and it doesn't act out of emotion or react differently depending on one's actions or feelings. It just is.

Q: Do you feel that it's possible to replicate that state of unconditional love here, in this physical realm?

A: Each of us, at our core, already *is* pure and unconditional love. However, when we express it here in this physical realm, we filter it through the mind, and it then expresses itself as human emotions.

The best metaphor I can think of to illustrate this is the example of white light *passing through* a prism. Unconditional love is like pure, white light. When you shine it through a prism, it refracts into all the different colors of the rainbow. These represent our emotions—joy, love, anxiety, envy, compassion, hate, empathy, and so on.

Each of us is like a prism, refracting pure white light (love) into all the different colors of the rainbow, and all of the hues (emotions) are equally needed for the whole. Few people, if any, would ever bring moral judgment against any given color. We wouldn't say, "Oh, that color is evil," or "That color is sinful." But we do this to people and their expressions of emotion, seeing some feelings as right and others as wrong.

When we judge some of our emotions as being negative and try to deny them, we're suppressing part of who we are. This creates a blockage within us and prevents us from expressing the fullness of our magnificence, just as extracting certain colors from the spectrum on the basis of a moral judgment would truncate the light and make it something it really isn't.

We don't have to act on every emotion; we just have to accept that they're part of who we are. Denying them would be like prohibiting a certain color from being refracted through the prism. Only by embracing the full spectrum of our feelings without judgment, can we get in touch with the pure essence of unconditional love that resides at our core.

Q: Is it your opinion that before we take physical form, we're already magnificent beings completely aware of who we truly are? If so, how does our magnificence get eroded and our sense of self become so damaged when we come into this life?

A: I'll tell you what I feel, but I think it will only raise more questions than answers! It seemed to me that we aren't meant to forget who we are, and that life isn't meant to be so difficult. It felt as though *we* made it tough here with our misplaced ideas and beliefs.

The internal understanding I received in that realm came as sort of an "imprint," but if I put a voice to it, here's what I would have been saying internally in that state: *Ooh, so life isn't supposed to be such a struggle—we're supposed to enjoy it and have fun! I wish I'd known this! Oh, so my body created the cancer because of all my dumb thoughts, judgments about myself, limiting beliefs, all of which caused me so much internal turmoil. Boy, if only I'd known that we're just supposed to come here and feel good about ourselves and about life—just express ourselves and have fun with it!*

Now this part is a little hard to explain, but let me try. I had a question that was something like this: *Why did something so big— like this terminal cancer thing—happen to me just for not realizing my own magnificence?*

Simultaneously, I had this understanding: *Ooh, I see—it didn't happen to me, because in truth, I'm never a victim. The cancer is just my own unexpressed power and energy! It turned inward against my body, rather than outward.*

I knew it wasn't a punishment or anything like that. It was just my own life force expressing itself as cancer because I didn't allow it to manifest as the magnificent, powerful force of Anita. I was aware that I had a choice as to whether I wanted to come back into my body or go onward into death. The cancer would no longer be there because the energy was no longer expressing itself that way but was going to be present as my infinite self.

I came back with the understanding that heaven truly is a state and not a place, and I've found that bliss has followed me here to Earth. I know this sounds really strange, but I even feel that our "true home" is also only a way of being and not a location. Right now, I feel that I'm home. I have no desire to be anywhere else. It makes no difference to me now whether I'm here or in the other realm. It's all just different parts of the experience of our greater, expanded, infinite, magnificent self. Our real home is within each of us and follows us wherever we go.

Q: Since I haven't had an NDE myself, is there a way to build up and maintain trust in the incredible life force that you speak of?

A: Absolutely. It's not necessary to have an NDE to realize your magnificence.

My experience taught me that the best way to build up and maintain trust and a feeling of connection with Universal life-force energy is from within. It starts by loving and trusting myself. The more I'm able to do so, the more centered I feel in the cosmic tapestry. The more connected each of us feels, the more we're able to touch others, enabling them to feel the same.

Q: What part in your healing and recovery did your belief system or faith play, if any, and how have your beliefs changed since then?

A: Absolutely no faith in anything was required for my healing. Rather, I'd say that it was the complete suspension of all previously held beliefs, doctrines, and dogma that caused my body to heal itself. In my case, the NDE was the catalyst.

From my point of view, strongly held ideas actually work against me. Having concrete beliefs limits my life experiences because they keep me locked into only what I know, and my knowledge in this world is limited by my physical senses. Being comfortable with uncertainty, on the other hand, opens me up to all possibilities. Ambiguity is wide open to infinite potential.

Needing certainty shackles my potential for the unexpected. Feeling *I don't know,* or *Let's see what happens,* allows my expanded self to provide answers and solutions that may be completely serendipitous and outrageously synchronistic. When I step into the realm of ambiguity I'm really at my most powerful. Letting go of all previous beliefs, disbeliefs, dogma, and doctrines puts the infinite universe at my disposal and works to give me the best possible outcome for my life. This is where I receive the most internal clarity. It's where magic happens.

Letting go of all previous attachments is an embrace of freedom and shows trust in my own divinity and magnificence. This, too, is a form of healing. When I release the need to heal physically, life becomes more free, whole, and enjoyable.

Q: Do you feel that your faith in the Source was a factor in your healing?

A: In my experience, I *became* the Source, and there was total clarity. There was no source outside of my own expanded awareness. It felt as though I encompassed totality. As I've mentioned, no faith in anything was needed for my healing because in that state, there's total clarity, and it felt as though everything became known. Belief or faith gave way to "knowing." It seemed that I became everything—I existed in everything and it all existed within me. I became eternal and infinite.

I awoke into this clarity, so I just understood. I knew that if I chose to return, my body would be healed. Because of the nature of my experience, my sense is that at our core, we're all One. We all come from Unity into separation, and then return to the Whole. I feel that my NDE was a glimpse of that Oneness. I could refer to it as *God,* or *Source,* or *Brahman,* or the *All That Is,* but I think different people have different ideas about what it means. I don't perceive the Divine as a separate entity from myself or anyone else. To me, it's a state of being rather than a separate being. It transcends duality so that I'm permanently united from within and am indivisible from it. My physical expression is just a facet of this Whole.

Q: Is there a place where our personal will and the will of the Whole connect so that we can access that place of healing and power freely?

A: I like to think that yes, it's possible for everyone to access that place of healing power freely. I believe that it's our collective mythologies—the stories we've been telling ourselves for generations—that prevent us from doing so. I think that this accumulation of beliefs is what's causing much of the disconnection and discord we perceive in the world, including within our own bodies.

We carry these invisible memes that keep us disconnected from our truth, causing us to believe that we're separate from

167

Universal energy. We remain stuck in duality, apart from our own creative center. We're the force that's not only forging, but also driving these myths. And as our stories shift, our physical reality reflects that shift.

In order to see this kind of healing more frequently, we need to evolve our mythologies and transform our memes to ones that let us realize that *we're One with Universal Energy*. This will allow us to feel connected to our creative center at all times and will facilitate more positive energy all around.

Healing takes place when our personal creative intent willfully converges with the Universal life force energy and sees it as One.

Q: Have you felt any sense of freedom since your NDE, and if so, how would you describe it?

A: I do feel liberated. I feel that my NDE not only freed me from my previously held ideologies, beliefs, and concepts, but also liberated me from the need to seek out new ones.

It seems to me we look for and hold onto these doctrines because they reassure us during uncertain times. However, we're prone to becoming dependent on them, needing them to be true in order to experience the comfort of certainty. I feel the more entrenched our beliefs about the limited nature of reality, the more we're actually perpetuating what they say.

My experience gave me a glimpse into what it feels like to be set free from the need for both physical and psychological certainty. In other words, it was possible for me to feel perfection even amidst ambiguity. Maintaining that level of mental liberation is true freedom for me.

Q: Do you think you would have chosen to return to this life if you'd known that your ill health would persist?

A: Because of the state of clarity I was in, I suspect that I would have come back with an understanding about why I felt the pull to return and express through a sick body. Hopefully, that knowledge would have eliminated or reduced my internal suffering, even if not the physical illness. There would have been a sense of purpose in having to live with a sick body. I believe everyone has a purpose, regardless of their physical condition.

Q: Your message comes through loud and clear that we should all *Be who we are!* But what about criminals and murderers? Should they also be who they are? Plus, you said that there's no judgment on the other side. That means we can actually get away with murder!

A: There's absolutely no condemnation in that realm, because there's nothing to condemn—we're all pure consciousness.

A lot of people don't like to hear that there's no judgment after we die. It's comforting to think that people will be held accountable for their wrongdoings. But punishment, rewards, judgment, condemnation, and the like are a "here" thing, not a "there" thing. That's why we have laws, rules, and systems.

On the other side, there's total clarity about why we are the way we are and why we did anything we did, no matter how unethical it felt in life. I believe that those who hurt others only do so out of their own pain and their feelings of limitation and separation. Perpetrators of acts such as rape and murder are far removed from even having an inkling of their own magnificence. I imagine they have to be extremely unhappy within themselves to cause so much pain to others, so in fact, they need the most compassion—not judgment and further suffering in the afterlife.

I actually don't believe that criminals and murderers *are* "being who they are." I think that we turn to destruction only when we've lost our way and drifted far from knowing the truth of who we really are. Criminals have lost their center, and what they're doing to others is actually a reflection of how they feel inside about themselves. We like to think of perpetrators and victims as "them" and "us," but there is no "them." It's *all* us!

A serial killer is diseased, similar to a person with cancer. And if we have more murderers in the world today, it means we have a sick society. Locking them away may have short-term benefits, just like treating the symptoms of cancer. However, if we don't transform and transcend the core issues within any society, the problem will only grow, requiring us to build more prisons and straining the judicial systems. Perpetrators are more than just victims of their own circumstances. They're the physical symptoms of underlying issues with *us as a whole.*

I'm not condoning their acts. I'm just trying to say that the knowledge of my own magnificence changed me. I think that if everyone were able to get in touch with their own truth and know their greatness, they wouldn't choose to be harmful. A happy and loved person who feels inseparable from Oneness knows that to injure another is the same as injuring the self.

Q: Are you saying that a criminal—say, a murderer—would go to the same place and feel the same nonjudgment as a saint?

A: Yes, that's what I'm saying.

In that state, we understand that everything we've done—no matter how seemingly negative—has actually come from fear, pain, and limited perspectives. A lot of what we do or feel is because we know no other way. Once we're in the other realm, however, our physical limitations become clear to us, so we're able to understand why we did things and we feel only compassion.

It felt as though those whom we label "perpetrators" are also victims of their own limitations, pain, and fear. When we realize this, we feel only connection with everyone and everything. I understood that in the other realm, we're all One. We're all the same.

If everyone knew this, we wouldn't need laws and prisons. But here, we don't understand, so we think in terms of "us" and "them," causing us to operate out of fear. This is why we have judgment, laws, prisons, and punishment. In this realm, at this time, we need them for our own protection. But on the other side, there's no such thing as punishment, because once we're there, we become aware that we're all connected.

Q: If we create our reality, do you think people will be punished for what they do through karma?

A: As I mentioned before, there is no punishment in the NDE state. I view karma as being more a concept of balance rather than cause and effect. For example, I would never use the phrase *bad karma,* as I don't believe there is such a thing. I simply believe all aspects of life are needed to create the whole.

Neither do I believe anymore that we live out all our lives sequentially in linear time, which is the framework that many people have for their ideas about karma. It's what I was brought up to think as well.

In the NDE state, however, I realized that every moment in all our lives—past, present, future, known, unknown, and unknowable—exist simultaneously, as though outside of what we know as time. I became aware that I already was everything I was trying to attain, and I believe that's true for everyone. All things that we perceive as positive, negative, good, or bad are simply parts of the perfect, balanced Whole.

Q. I've heard people speak of the importance of forgiveness. Did you find that you had to do a lot of forgiving in the other realm?

A: In the NDE state, the clarity is so acute that the whole concept of forgiveness takes on a very different meaning. I realized that it was *myself* I hadn't forgiven, not other people. There was no negative judgment for anything I'd seemingly done wrong—I felt only understanding about why I'd done everything.

I also realized that within that infinite, nonjudgmental realm, there's actually no need to forgive myself or anybody else. We're all perfect, exquisite children of the universe, and we exist out of pure love. Unconditional love is our birthright, not judgment or condemnation, and there's nothing we need to do to earn it. This is simply who and what we are.

The need to forgive is born out of seeing things as good and bad, but when there's no judgment, there's nothing for us to pardon. Within the cosmic tapestry we're creating, all thoughts, words, and deeds are necessary for the creation of the infinite, magnificent Whole. Just as with the light spectrum I mentioned earlier, all colors are needed to give contrast and bring life into being. What's to forgive?

At this point, I've replaced forgiveness with empathy, unconditional love, and compassion—for myself and for others. Rather than judge, creating a need for pardon, I now have only caring and great respect for the multifaceted role each of us plays in the Whole of creation

Q: Wouldn't too much self-love make people selfish and egotistical?

A: Once we understand that each of us is at the heart of the infinite universe, our centrality to the Whole becomes paramount, and we see the value in loving the self. We can't give what we don't have.

In my culture, I was taught to put others first and myself last or not at all. I wasn't taught to love myself or to value who and what I am. As a consequence, I had very little to offer others. Only when we fill our own cup with regard for ourselves, will we have any to give away. Only when we love ourselves unconditionally, accepting ourselves as the magnificent creatures we are with great respect and compassion, can we ever hope to offer the same to anyone else. Cherishing the self comes first, and caring for others is the inevitable outcome.

Selfishness comes from too little self-love, not too much, as we compensate for our lack. There's no such thing as caring for the self too much, just as there's no such thing as too much genuine affection for others. Our world suffers from too little self-love and too much judgment, insecurity, fear, and mistrust. If we all cared about ourselves more, most of these ills would disappear.

To say "I love you" when I have no matching emotion for myself is playacting. It's not real. Affection for the self and others is the same thing. We're all One—all interconnected. Having an awareness of our own divinity can help us to see our magnificence and worthiness for love without conditions. Once we understand this, offering the same to everyone else becomes much easier.

Q: Most people on a spiritual path believe that the ego impedes spiritual growth and that we're supposed to shed the ego. Why aren't you advocating this?

A: Because if you deny the ego, it will push back against you harder. The more you reject something, the more it fights back for its own survival. But when you can completely love your ego unconditionally and accept it as part of how you express in this life, you'll no longer have a problem with it. It won't impede your growth—on the contrary, it will be an asset.

We're all born with an ego—it's a natural part of who we are here. We're only completely without it in death. Fighting against this during life only creates more self-judgment. Plus, only when we love our ego unconditionally are we able to accept everyone else's. This is when it stops being an issue, and your humility and magnificence really shine through.

Q: What's your opinion on service and serving others?

A: When service comes from the center of our being, it's the highest form of self-love. We know this is the case when we feel joy while serving. It will even feel light and fun! This uplifts both us and the recipient and helps to elevate the receiver's self worth.

But if we perform out of an obligation or sense of duty, it feels serious and heavy and can be energy draining. This really doesn't do us any good, and it's not that great for the recipient either—especially if they can sense that we're acting out of obligation. This can make the receiver feel small and worthless.

In addition, when something comes from the center of our being, it's no longer an action—it becomes who we are. We don't need to think about it or work at it. We become an instrument for service to manifest on this planet. This is the difference between *being of service* and *performing a service*.

This connected level comes with the realization that there's no separation between the self and the Universe. It's the knowledge that what I do for the Whole, I'm also doing for the self, and vice versa—and that's truly a joyful and fun state to be in!

Q: As I look around, it seems to me a lot of rancor, arguments, and downright hostility come from everyone insisting that their reality or point of view is the only one. Yet your experience and those of many others who've had NDEs indicate that what we consider reality is no more or less real than a sort of dream. So essentially, people are arguing over whose illusion is the most valid. Can you elaborate on this?

A: I can only recount my experience. For me, it felt as though when I "died," I woke up from a dream. It didn't feel as if I went anywhere, but as though I'd awakened and had omni-perceptual senses—that is, 360-degree vision and complete *synesthesia,* or simultaneous perception of the senses. I could see, hear, feel, and know *everything* that pertained to me! I was living my past, present, and future simultaneously. I also knew what was going on beyond walls and space, as long as it related to me—hence the visuals of my doctors' conversations, my brother on the plane, and so on.

I sort of liken it to a blind person being able to see for the first time. The individual didn't go anywhere, but the clarity of what the world actually looks like (as opposed to what he thought it was like) would be amazing! He would suddenly understand things such as color and shade. These would previously have been beyond his conceptual understanding.

In that respect, for me, there was this incredible knowledge of how we're all interconnected and how what I feel affects the universe, for the Whole is within me. As far as I'm concerned, if I'm happy, the Universe is happy. If I love myself, everyone else will love me, too, and so on.

After coming back, even though I've lost some of the enhanced senses that I had during the NDE, the understanding, clarity, and feelings of love haven't left me. The dots are already connected, and I can't go back to thinking the way I used to. Imagine the blind person going back to being blind. Every time he makes his way through the world, he knows what it really looks like, even though he cannot see it. That's sort of how it feels for me now.

As for this plane not being real, I feel that we've each created our own reality based on what we think the world is like. In that awakened state, it felt as though this 3-D existence is just a culmination of my thoughts. When I went to the other realm, I actually woke up to a place more real than this one . . . sort of how it feels when we awaken from a dream into our everyday reality!

Q: What are your thoughts on religion? I notice that you rarely, if ever, bring it up when you speak about your experience.

A: That's because death transcends religion, which is something we've created in order to help us to live or to help us understand death. But once I experienced the other realm, trying to make it fit into a religion—no matter which one—actually seemed to reduce it.

Another reason I don't really talk about it is because religion can be divisive, and that's never my intention. I much prefer to be inclusive. I experienced us as all being One, knowing that when we die, we'll all go to the same place. To me, it doesn't matter whether you believe in Jesus, Buddha, Shiva, Allah, or none of the above. What matters is how you *feel about yourself,* right here and right now, because that's what determines how you conduct your life *here.* There's no time except the present moment, so it's important to be yourself and live your own truth. Passionate scientists living from their magnificence are as valuable to humankind as a whole room full of Mother Teresas.

Q: One of the most intriguing statements you've made about what you understood from your experience has implications that are profound, multifaceted, and far-reaching. I'm thinking

of your contention that we can effectively alter our past by the moment-to-moment choices we make as our lives unfold into the future. Am I reading too much into what you're expressing, or is this close to what you understand?

A: You've interpreted it absolutely as I meant it. I feel that the present moment is the only point in time we have to create our reality. Please note that I intentionally don't say "create our future." The past and future felt fluid to me, and this is how I was able to alter the test results depending on whether I came back or not.

I agree that this is important because of its implications. For me, it continues to unfold each day, and now this awareness has become bigger than the NDE itself.

Q: In your NDE narrative, you stated, "All disease first begins in the energy first, and then manifests in the body." Do you have any sense as to how this is accomplished and what prompts the disease to form in the first place?

A: During my NDE, I felt as though my body, in its solid form, didn't exist. I was just pure energy—perhaps this could be interpreted as the soul or the spirit. It was much bigger than the body, and I like to use the word *magnificent,* because that's how I felt in that state. It was almost as if having a physical self was an afterthought. This infinite energy mass was the real me, and the body was only a barometer to show how much of this life force was "coming through" or being expressed. It felt as if the 3-D world was the other dimension, and my energy mass was real.

From this, I feel that when we say people are of a higher vibration, we probably mean that they're letting more of their authentic magnificence come through, so their "barometer" readings are really high! Consequently their positive energy and physical presence are strong. In that realm, however, nobody seemed stronger or weaker. Everyone was magnificent. But how much of that we express through our bodies into this dimension seems to be our choice.

Q: Are you suggesting that the power of your healing came internally and not from an external source?

A: It was neither internal nor external, or I could say it was both. Once I was no longer expressing from the state of duality, I realized that there's no separation between within and without. I became the Source of all things, and the Source became me. But if you're referring to whether I think it's me—as in the ego or the physical self—behind my healing, then no. It emanated from expressing through my infinite self and knowing that I'm not separate from source or anything.

Q: What are your thoughts on the different healing modalities, both Western and Eastern?

A: I feel that many treatments and modalities are useful—and I also want to be clear that I don't think it's necessary to have an NDE to heal.

Before my NDE, everything I did came from a place of fear, even when it came to healing. My psychological makeup was such that I only sought out these things because I was afraid of the consequences of not doing so.

But when the dread is no longer there, and we come from a perspective of trust, then the healing modalities stand a much better chance of working. During my short stint in India, my health improved because I was away from the atmosphere of fear. I was in a culture that supported an entirely different outlook on cancer, one that was much more positive. In Westernized Hong Kong, most people I encountered had enormous fear of cancer and passed that on to me. But in India, I was given a different perspective, which gave me hope. I put trust in it, and I felt the effects on my health quite rapidly.

Q: You said that your cancer seemed to heal when you went to India and received ayurvedic treatments, but when you returned to Hong Kong, the disease came back. Do you

have any thoughts as why the cancer seemed to disappear in India, but returned in Hong Kong?

A: To reiterate, I think ayurveda worked for me in India because there was no conflict. Everyone around me believed in the same thing, and what I was doing made sense to everyone. I wasn't confused. For the first time, I felt I was on the right path. There was also a lot of support in terms of ayurvedic doctors, ashrams, and so on, all of which supported this modality.

But here in Hong Kong, the choices are endless and multicultural, and all the different modalities conflict with each other! My first choice has never been conventional Western medicine, but if I hadn't been inclined toward other methods, I would have chosen it. Personally, however, it was the last thing I wanted.

I think if I'd been born and brought up in the middle of China, traditional Chinese medicine would have worked for me, too—but then I might not even have gotten sick in the first place! Do you know that in Chinese culture, cancer is often referred to as "Western people's disease"? Are you aware that the incidence of cancer in China, Japan, and even India is far lower than in Western countries?

Some people think it's because of diet, but I feel that's only part of it. Another, possibly even larger factor may be mind-set—the Western belief in cancer, the fear of it, and the constant "awareness" campaigns! Conventional western medicine focuses on detecting cancer, and most of their technology is diagnostic rather than promoting overall physical well-being and balance.

Q: What differences did you experience between Eastern and Western healing approaches?

A: Going to and fro between the two caused my emotional state to swing between fear and hope.

The Western doctors focused only on the cancer, making me feel as though something external was attacking my body and it had to be gotten rid off. In other words, cancer is the enemy and has to be attacked. Their diagnosis always instilled fear.

Eastern doctors (from both ayurveda and Traditional Chinese Medicine) looked at my well-being more holistically. They viewed my illness as my body's way of trying to heal from its imbalances— not just physical ones, but emotional and mental as well. The cancer was actually my ally. These methods were much more comforting and gave me more hope.

Post-NDE, it's easier for me to see that the cancer itself wasn't the enemy or the disease. I know what it was trying to tell me, and in my case, it *was* in fact my body's way of trying to heal me. For me, viewing cancer as an enemy that needed to be annihilated didn't get rid of the underlying problem that caused it in the first place. Something deeper was addressed during the NDE, triggering the cancer cells to disappear.

Q: You seem to be saying that healing approaches are all culturally based and that there's no intrinsic superiority of one modality over another when it comes to cancer. Do I understand you correctly?

A: Yes. This is essentially what I'm saying, based on my experience. Remember, from my perspective, many modern-day illnesses are actually mental and spiritual diseases that manifest in the body. Treatment that addresses the mind and spirit will have a much better chance of effecting change than an approach that merely deals with the body. And any modality that's wholeheartedly supported by the surrounding culture will be more effective than one without such underlying strength—especially if the method addresses the patient's mind-set and spiritual outlook.

Q: Since your own experience, what are your thoughts on cancer and medicine? Do you think we'll get any closer to finding a cure for cancer?

A: Personally, simply because of my own experience, I believe that specific cases such as mine are a disease of the mind and the soul, not the body. The physical manifestation is merely a symptom of something much deeper. I don't believe that the cure for these cases lies in medicine, because scientists look in all the wrong places—they're only studying the symptoms, not the cause, and then creating drugs to mask the symptoms. They may be able to manage the symptoms, but I don't believe they'll find a "cure."

It seems to me that there's a very rich field of inquiry surrounding the disease, based on what I understood from my own illness and NDE. Yet sadly, I haven't seen any real well-funded research on what I view as the real causes of cancer, while billions of dollars are spent on drug-based approaches. I often wonder whether it's easier to make money selling medication than it is to bolster people's sense of their own divine magnificence!

I believe that *my* cancer was related to my self-identity, and it feels as though it was my body's way of telling me that my soul was grieving for the loss of its own worth—of its identity. If I'd known the truth of who I *actually* am, I wouldn't have gotten cancer!

Q: What's your opinion about money from the perspective of the afterlife? Some believe that money is the cause of a lot of the problems and evil in this world. What do you think?

A: Money in and of itself has no power other than what we choose to give it, and it's the same with everything in this dimension. Anything can be used for good or bad, but in and of itself, it's just neutral. We choose to give it power. We put our judgments (both negative and positive) onto money, religion, race, and so on. We create certain beliefs about them, give them an emotional charge, and presto, we've created a situation where people either become stronger or fight in defense.

I'm not saying that this is a bad thing—it may even be a necessary part of existing in this realm. We live in a world of seeming duality, where we're always deciding what's bad or good, what's negative or positive. We have emotions, and we put them into our beliefs, including those about money. We could have given those same emotional charges to something else, another commodity or system of exchange, and that would hold the same power that money currently does.

But death transcends duality. It transcends religion, race, culture, and all our values and beliefs. We aren't any of those things, but are merely expressing through them at this point in time. We're something far, far greater.

Q: Many who would like to heal themselves want to know how to go about things like "trusting in your own healing," "letting go and allowing healing," and "accessing your place of healing." Are these platitudes of any use to the average person? People who want to heal their bodies need to know how to put such things into practice.

A: I don't like to advocate a set methodology, instructions, or anything like that, because if I do, I'm only creating more dogma, and the whole point is to be free of that. I do suggest, however, not viewing illness or symptoms as "something to be gotten rid of," like an enemy. This a fear-based reaction. For me, the appearance of these symptoms is my body's way of trying to heal me. I know that if I try to eliminate the illness with an adversarial attitude, I end up doing the opposite, antagonizing it and embedding myself deeper into the illness mind-set.

This doesn't necessarily mean that you don't go and see a doctor. I'm purely referring to how I view disease or physical manifestations of the body. The idea is not to obsess about it and have your days revolve around doing things for the sole purpose of getting rid of the illness. It's actually far more productive to distract yourself and stay occupied with activities that stimulate you in a positive, creative way.

As far as I could, I'd try to free myself from needing my health to be a certain way in order to find happiness and just create joy in the moment, as though I were already healthy. Living in the present means not carrying any emotional baggage from one segment of time into the next. Every instant is unique and can't be replicated. It's our choice whether to carry our fears with us, keeping us stuck in illness.

You don't have to be a spiritual guru or anything. Just make the most of every minute, living it to the fullest and doing things that make you happy, whether you have a month to live or 100 years.

Q: Theories are interesting, but what about practical advice? How do you stay healthy now—what do you eat and what do you avoid in your diet?

A: Well, my diet *has* changed since my NDE, but I'm afraid it's not in the way you think! I used to be paranoid about what I ate. I was a strict vegetarian. I consumed only organic foods and was into macrobiotics, vitamin supplements, and wheatgrass juice—and that was before I got sick. I thought that everything caused cancer, from microwaves to preservatives. I used to eat very healthfully, but I did so out of fear.

Now I eat whatever I'm drawn to. I enjoy chocolate and a good wine or champagne from time to time. I just make sure that I have a good time with food and life! I think that it's more important to be happy than anything else.

It's no fun eating all the so-called right foods out of fear of getting sick and being miserable about it. Being anxious causes a whole other set of problems. Our bodies are actually a lot more resilient than we give them credit for, particularly if we're happy and not under stress.

Even when I choose to eat healthfully, I do so out of love instead of fear. That's my method in every aspect of my life, and I invite you to live the same way.

Q: If there were a message or lesson from your NDE that you wish everyone could know or understand, something that you wish you could shout out from the rooftops, what would that be?

A: I would want you to know that *every* part of you is magnificent—your ego, intellect, body, and spirit. It's who you are—a beautiful product of this Universe's creation. Every aspect of you is perfect. There's nothing to let go, nothing to forgive, nothing to attain. You already are everything you need to be. It can seem so complicated, but it's not.

If a religion makes you feel lesser than its deities, then you've either misinterpreted it or it's not doing a good job of teaching you the truth. If a guru, teacher, or master makes you feel that you aren't "yet" enlightened and still have more to "learn," "release," or "let go of" before getting there, then they're not doing a good job of teaching you who you truly are, or you're misunderstanding them.

Remind everyone close to you to be themselves, and tell them that you love them just the way they are! They're perfect and so are you. There's nothing not to love. Most suffering stems from feeling "less than." You aren't less than anything or anyone! You are complete.

The *only thing* you need to learn is that you already *are* what you're seeking to attain. Just express your uniqueness *fearlessly*, with abandon! That's why you're made the way you are, and that's why you're here in the physical world.

❧ *Afterword* ❧

Before I close, I'd like to leave you with a few final words. Always remember not to give away your power—instead, get in touch with your own magnificence. When it comes to finding the right path, there's a different answer for each person. The only universal solution I have is to love yourself unconditionally and be yourself fearlessly! This is the most important lesson I learned from my NDE, and I honestly feel that if I'd always known this, I never would have gotten cancer in the first place.

When we're true to ourselves, we become instruments of truth for the planet. Because we're all connected, we touch the lives of everyone around us, who then affect others. Our only obligation is to be the love we are and allow our answers to come from within in the way that's most appropriate for us.

Finally, I can't stress enough how important it is to enjoy yourself and not take yourself or life too seriously. One of the biggest flaws with many traditional spiritual systems is that they often make us take life too seriously. Although you know that I abhor creating doctrines, if I ever had to create a set of tenets for a spiritual path to healing, number one on my list would be to make sure to laugh as often as possible throughout every single day—and preferably laugh at myself. This would be hands down over and above any form of prayer, meditation, chanting, or diet reform. Day-to-day problems never seem as big when viewed through a veil of humor and love.

In this age of information technology, we're bombarded with news seemingly at the speed of light. We're living in an age of high stress and fear, and in the midst of trying to protect ourselves from everything we think is "out there," we've forgotten to enjoy ourselves and to take care of what's inside.

Our life is our prayer. It's our gift to this universe, and the memories we leave behind when we someday exit this world will be our legacy to our loved ones. We owe it to ourselves and to everyone around us to be happy and to spread that joy around.

If we can go through life armed with humor and the realization that we are love, we'll already be ahead of the game. Add a box of good chocolates into the mix, and we've really got a winning formula!

I wish you joy as you realize your magnificence and express yourself fearlessly in the world.

— Namaste!
Anita Moorjani

ᕙᓂ *Acknowledgments* ᓂᕙ

To me, this is possibly the most important part of the book. This is where I get to express my gratitude to everyone who, in some way or another, is integral to this work coming about. Some were directly involved in its manifestation, and others indirectly, but all have played a major part in my journey from there to here.

To Dr. Wayne W. Dyer—what can I say? Your generosity of spirit continues to leave me speechless—and that doesn't happen often! I know that the universe conspired to bring us together even before we were aware of it, at the perfect time. You're such an intrinsic part of my journey, and I couldn't have accomplished this without you. Your kindness and advice along the way have meant a lot to me, and it's no wonder that the world is inspired by you. *Thank you, thank you, thank you,* from the bottom of my heart for opening the door for me to share my story with the world and for making my life so magical. But most of all, *thank you for being you.* I love you dearly!

To my best friend and soul brother, Rio Cruz—whatever I say in gratitude sounds trite and doesn't even come close to how I feel about our friendship. During these years, you've been such an integral influence in my life, helping me along as I tried to fit into a world that wasn't always ready to hear what I had to share. Your vast knowledge of NDEs brought me tremendous comfort, and your unyielding support when others challenged me kept me sane; and I can't thank you enough for that. You're my best friend and believed from day one that my story needed to be shared with the world. Thank you for gently nudging me throughout the journey of this book, encouraging me to finally bring it to its fruition. I love you mucho, amigo!

To Mira Kelley—you are such a beautiful soul! Thank you so much for being part of the synchronicity and for bringing my story to Dr. Dyer's attention. Your actions actually brought the theory of allowing to fruition. I love you!

To Jessica Kelley, my editor—thank you so much for helping to bring my story alive on these pages. I'm so grateful for your patience and for always being so astute in understanding what I was trying to say. You were fantastic to work with. Thank you!

To Reid Tracy, Shannon Littrell, and everyone at Hay House—thank you for your support! I'm so thrilled to be part of the Hay House family.

To Dr. Jeffrey Long, owner of Near Death Experience Research Foundation—thank you for recognizing the importance of my message, for posting my experience on the home page of your website, and bringing it to the attention of the world.

To Dr. Peter Ko—I'm so grateful to you for taking an interest in my case and flying to Hong Kong to meet me and research my medical records. Thank you for your perseverance and all your great detective work in going through that huge pile of medical records and files!

To Dr. Brian Walker, our family doctor and friend—I know I gave you a scare! Thank you for not giving up on me and for being there for all of us through those difficult days.

To the wonderful team of doctors and caregivers at the Hong Kong Sanatorium who saw me through my darkest hours—thank you for allowing the universe to do its work through your hands.

To my beautiful NDERF family—you've been my community, my family, and my friends for the last five years. Thank you Dave Thaler, Lucas Tailor, Mark Sweeney, Alison Bruer, Bailey Struss, Cloe Solis, Dave Maswarey, Don O'Connor, Wayne Hart, Carla Dobel, and Lorraine. I couldn't have survived this journey without all of you, as you provided me with a community where I felt like I belonged and gave me so many laughs along the way. I really adore all of you!

And finally, to my beautiful family—my brother Anoop, who means the world to me; his family, Mona and Shahn; and my dear mother, whose love for me has always been unwavering and unconditional. I love you, dear Mother, and am sorry I put you through so much pain. And last but not least, to my darling husband—I'm so blessed to have you in my life and trust that you'll always know how much I love you. I treasure what we have with all my heart and hope that we may be together for all our lives. I love you, darling.

✑ *About the Author* ✑

Anita Moorjani was born in Singapore of Indian parents, moved to Hong Kong at the age of two, and has lived in Hong Kong most of her life. Because of her background and British education, she is multilingual and grew up speaking English, Cantonese, and an Indian dialect simultaneously; she later learned French at school. Anita had been working in the corporate world for many years before being diagnosed with cancer in April 2002. Her fascinating and moving near-death experience in early 2006 tremendously changed her perspective on life, and her work is now ingrained with the depths and insights she gained while in the other realm.

As a result of her near-death experience, Anita is often invited to speak at conferences and events around the globe to share her insights. She's also a frequent guest at the University of Hong Kong's department of behavioral sciences, speaking on topics such as dealing with terminal illness, facing death, and the psychology of spiritual beliefs. She is the embodiment of the truth that we all have the inner power and wisdom to overcome even life's most adverse situations, as she's the living proof of this possibility.

Anita currently lives in Hong Kong with her husband, and when she's not traveling and speaking at conferences, she works as an intercultural consultant for multinational corporations based in the city.

Website: **www.anitamoorjani.com**

∽ NOTES ∾

～ NOTES ～

NOTES

We hope you enjoyed this Hay House book. If you'd like to receive our online catalog featuring additional information on Hay House books and products, or if you'd like to find out more about the Hay Foundation, please contact:

Hay House, Inc., P.O. Box 5100, Carlsbad, CA 92018-5100
(760) 431-7695 or (800) 654-5126
(760) 431-6948 (fax) or (800) 650-5115 (fax)
www.hayhouse.com® • **www.hayfoundation.org**

Published and distributed in Australia by: Hay House Australia Pty. Ltd.,
18/36 Ralph St., Alexandria NSW 2015
Phone: 612-9669-4299 • *Fax:* 612-9669-4144 • www.hayhouse.com.au

Published and distributed in the United Kingdom by: Hay House UK, Ltd.,
292B Kensal Rd., London W10 5BE
Phone: 44-20-8962-1230 • *Fax:* 44-20-8962-1239 • www.hayhouse.co.uk

Published and distributed in the Republic of South Africa by: Hay House SA
(Pty), Ltd., P.O. Box 990, Witkoppen 2068
Phone/Fax: 27-11-467-8904 • www.hayhouse.co.za

Published in India by: Hay House Publishers India,
Muskaan Complex, Plot No. 3, B-2, Vasant Kunj, New Delhi 110 070
Phone: 91-11-4176-1620 • *Fax:* 91-11-4176-1630 • www.hayhouse.co.in

Distributed in Canada by: Raincoast,
9050 Shaughnessy St., Vancouver, B.C. V6P 6E5
Phone: (604) 323-7100 • *Fax:* (604) 323-2600 • www.raincoast.com

Take Your Soul on a Vacation

Visit **www.HealYourLife.com®** to regroup,
recharge, and reconnect with your own magnificence.

Featuring blogs, mind-body-spirit news,
and life-changing wisdom from Louise Hay and friends.

Visit **www.HealYourLife.com** today!